MASTERS OF ART

THE STORY OF ARCHITECTURE

FRANCESCO MILO

◆

ILLUSTRATED BY
LORENZO CECCHI, STUDIO GALANTE, ANDREA RICCIARDI

PETER BEDRICK BOOKS
NEW YORK

DoGi

Produced by:
DoGi spa, Florence
Original title:
L'architettura
Text:
Francesco Milo
Editing:
Andrea Bachini
Illustration:
Simone Boni
Lorenzo Cecchi
Andrea Ricciardi
Studio L.R.Galante:
Manuela Cappon
Luigi Galante
Alessandro Menchi
Francesco Spadoni
Subject:
Francesco Lo Bello
Page design:
Sebastiano Ranchetti
Picture research:
Francesco Milo
Graphic design:
Oliviero Ciriaci
Art director:
Sebastiano Ranchetti
English translation:
Angela Whitehouse
Diane Melville
Editing, English-language edition:
Ruth Nason, Nathaniel Harris

© 1999 by DoGi spa
Florence, Italy

English language text © 1999 by
DoGi spa/Peter Bedrick Books

Published by
PETER BEDRICK BOOKS
156 Fifth Avenue,
10010 New York

Library of Congress
Cataloging-in-Publication Data
is available from
the Library of Congress
ISBN 0-87226-528-5

Printed in Italy in 1999

Photolitho:
Venanzoni DTP, Florence

♦ HOW THE INFORMATION IS PRESENTED

Some of the double pages in this book deal with a single period and with a particular style in the history of architecture, from the Paleolithic, through classical Greece and Rome, Romanesque and Gothic, Renaissance and Baroque, up until the 20th century. Some double pages deal with great national or continental cultures. And some concentrate on specific building techniques, such as arches and domes and prefabrication. In all cases, the most representative buildings have been chosen to illustrate each period, culture, or technique. The information about the main subject on each double page is supplemented with material about other significant historical and artistic events.

HINDU TEMPLES

♦ THE PAGE
The main theme of each double page, introduced in the top left paragraph, is shown in the large central illustration and the captions attached to it. Other text, photographs, and smaller drawings, grouped around the main illustration, provide further background information.

♦ CREDITS

The original and previously unpublished illustrations in this book may only be reproduced with the prior permission of Donati Giudici Associati, who hold the copyright.
Abbreviations: b, bottom; c, center; l, left; r, right; t, top.
ILLUSTRATIONS
The illustrations are by: Lorenzo Cecchi: pp. 14–15, 26–27, 42–43, 58–59; Andrea Ricciardi: pp. 12–13, 18–19, 34–35, 36–37, 38–39; Studio Galante: Manuela Cappon: pp. 24–25, 40–41, 46–47, 54–55; Luigi Galante: pp. 8–9, 48–49, 60–61; Alessandro Menchi: pp. 32–33, 44–45, 50–51, 62–63, 56–57; Alessandro Spadoni: pp. 10–11, 20–21, 22–23, 30–31, 52–53; Studio Inklink: Simone Boni: pp. 4–5, 6–7, 16–17; Giuseppe Arrighi: pp. 28–29
COVER ILLUSTRATION: front cover: Andrea Ricciardi; back cover: t: Boni/Galante; tr: Lorenzo Cecchi; b: Francesco Spadoni
FRONTISPIECE: Luigi Galante

PHOTOGRAPHS AND DOCUMENTS
DoGi spa has made every effort to trace other possible copyright holders. If any omissions or errors have been made, this will be corrected at reprint.
Inside
4. t: Giuseppe Arrighi; b: Boni/ Galante. **5.** Boni/Galante. **6.** Archivio Curcio. **7.** l: Aerofilms; r: Sergio Bottai. **8.** Giacinto Gaudenzi. **9.** l: Archivio Dogi; r: Francesco Lo Bello. **10.** Luigi Galante. **11.** tl: Archivio Dogi; t Igda, Milan; b: Siliotti. **12.** l: Igda, Milan; r: Ecole Nationale Supérieure de Beaux Arts, Paris. **13.** l: Sebastiano Ranchetti; c: Sebastiano Ranchetti; r: British Museum, London. **14.** l: Archivio Dogi; c: Fotostock, Barcelona; b: Sebastiano Ranchetti. **16.** Sebastiano Ranchetti. **17.** l: Giulia Anna Bernardini; r: Scala, Florence. **18.** Archivio White Star (Marcello Bertinetti). **19.** Boni/ Galante. **20.** t: L. Haghe; b:

Archivio Curcio. **21.** Archivio Curcio. **22.** Sebastiano Ranchetti. **23.** Laura Ottina. **24.** l: Archivio Dogi; r: Francesco Lo Bello. **25.** l: Tiziano Perotto; r: Lorenzo Cecchi. **26.** l: Archivio Dogi; r: Peter Willi, Paris. **27.** l: Sebastiano Ranchetti; r: Manuela Cappon. **28.** Giuseppe Arrighi. **29.** tl: Giuseppe Arrighi; bl: Sebastiano Ranchetti; tr: Sergio Bottai. **30.** tl: Archivio Dogi; tr: Archivio Dogi; b: Sebastiano Ranchetti. **32.** l: Archivio Dogi; r: Sebastiano Ranchetti. **34.** tl: Luigi Galante; tr: Sebastiano Ranchetti; b: Archivio Dogi. **35.** l: Lorenzo Cecchi and Francesco Petracchi; r: The Bridgeman Art Library, London. **36.** l: Scala, Florence; c: Sebastiano Ranchetti; r: Sebastiano Ranchetti. **37.** Claudia Saraceni. **39.** tl: Archivio Curcio; tr: Archivio Dogi; b: Scala, Florence. **40.** Lorenzo Cecchi. **41.** l: Zefa/Orion; r: Francesco Lo Bello. **42.** tl: Marco Rabatti; c: Giancarlo Gasponi; **43.** Archivio

Dogi. **44.** Boni/Galante. **45.** l: Forbidden City Museum, Peking; r: Rapho (G. Gerster). **47.** l: Archivio Dogi; r: Image Bank, London. **48.** Laura Ottina. **49.** l: Sime (J. Huber); r: Archivio Dogi. **51.** Archivio Electa. **52.** tl: Boni/Galante; tr: Boni/Galante. **53.** Carlo Cantini, Florence. **54.** Sebastiano Ranchetti. **55.** Paola Ghiggi. **56.** Renato Avril. **57.** Archivio Dogi. **58.** t: Imapress (S. Visalli); b: Archivio Electa. **60.** H. Roger-Viollet. **61.** Pino Dell'Aquila. **63.** Eamonn O'Mahony.
Cover
Clockwise from top left: Archivio Dogi; Fotoftock, Barcelona; Archivio Dogi; Sergio Bottai; Archivio Curcio; V; Imapress (S.Visalli); Archivio Curcio; V; Archivio Curcio; Sergio Bottai; V; Claudia Sareceni; Archivio Dogi; Igda, Milan; Archivio Dogi; Scala Florence; Archivio Dogi; Archivio Dogi; Sime (J. Huber); Rapho (H. Gersten); Agenzia Contrasto.

CONTENTS

WOOD

The first true buildings were made by Paleolithic hunter-gatherers, when they constructed shelters, instead of relying on the natural cover provided by caves and rock ledges. The material they used was wood. When forests covered most of the planet, wood could be found everywhere, and the early builders learned to exploit its useful qualities, which included resilience, lightness, and resistance to the elements. Some simple techniques, devised thousands of years ago to build in wood, are still in use today. For centuries, even when buildings were cased in stone or brick, the actual core was usually wood. Wood was arguably the single most important material in the history of architecture, absolutely irreplaceable until very recent times.

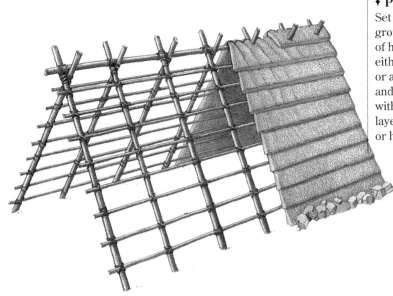

✦ **PRIMITIVE HUTS**
Set directly on the ground, this kind of hut or tent had either a rectangular or a circular base, and was covered with overlapping layers of reeds or hides.

✦ **PILE DWELLINGS**
Thousands of years ago, prehistoric people began to settle around lakes and rivers, where edible plants, game, and fish were plentiful. The first dwellings were raised on wooden piles, to avoid flooding.

✦ **THE FIRST ROADS**
Tree trunks were laid down and covered with thick layers of plant materials in order to make a safe, dry road across the swampy soil that often surrounded the lakes.

✦ **EARLY DEFENSIVE MEASURES**
Palisades were built around settlements in order to protect them from marauding outsiders and dangerous beasts.

✦ **TRADITIONAL HOMES**
In northern European countries, the same building techniques were used for centuries. Set on a brick foundation, the basic structure was built with timbers, which were held together by wooden pegs (and later nails) and carpentry. The areas between the beams were filled in with clay, mud, and bundles of twigs. Unlike stone, wood does not retain the cold and therefore provides a pleasant interior environment.

THE PITS ✦
Large pits were dug near the settlement, often to extract clay for building. They were then used as garbage dumps.

THE ADVANTAGES ♦ OF FLEXIBILITY
The traditional Japanese home was made entirely of timber. Slightly raised, like ancient pile dwellings, it had a low roof and a flexible structure, achieved by using bamboo. The interior partitions were made of paper. The structure's flexibility limited the damage caused by storms and earthquakes.

♦ THE ROOF
The roof was covered with bundles of rushes or similar materials. These placed little weight on the timber frame and could be renewed easily when they deteriorated. The overhang of the sloping roof also served to protect the outside walls of the building.

♦ THE HOUSE'S FRAMEWORK
The framework consisted of long beams fixed upright in the ground, attached to sets of horizontal beams – a remarkably stable arrangement.

♦ THE WALLS
Logs or intertwined branches filled in the gaps between the timber framing. They were held in place by a mixture of twigs and clay, which also served as insulation.

STONE

In the distant past, human beings built in stone whenever they wanted their creations to be permanent. Prehistoric European peoples raised huge structures which were almost certainly settings for, or linked with, their religious rituals. In fact, the most ancient forms of stone architecture, erected over 6,000 years ago, appeared in western Europe; notable examples were the tombs built by early farming communities in the Iberian peninsula (modern Spain and Portugal). The earthworks and stones of the British monument Stonehenge are particularly impressive. The monument seems to have had an astronomical function, no doubt connected with religious beliefs about the significance of the heavenly bodies. The number of stones and their orientation are said to correspond to the main phases of the moon and to the sun's position on the horizon at the point where the seasons changed.

⧫ TRILITHON
This is the most basic form of stone construction: two blocks are set up vertically and a third is placed horizontally across them. This example is near the Bisceglie chambered tomb, in Apulia, Italy, which dates from the 3rd millennium B.C.

THE BLUE STONES ⧫
These were the first stones to be set up in any number, eventually arranged to form an inner ring and horseshoe. Since they come from Wales, they must have been transported for almost 250 miles.

⧫ THE STONE CIRCLES
Stonehenge is the largest known circular grouping of upright stones and capstones. The main structures were built in three phases: first, the ditches and banks were dug; then the blue stones were erected; after this, from about 2000 B.C., most of the massive stone building was done. Impressive stone circles are found in many parts of the British Isles and Brittany.

BUILDING ⧫ TECHNIQUES
Sleds made of large tree trunks were used to move the enormous blocks of stone. At the site, they were lowered into specially dug ditches and levered into a vertical position. The horizontal blocks were raised on a temporary embankment or a wooden structure. This could only have been accomplished by a mass effort.

♦ **THE SARSEN CIRCLE**
The sarsen stones, which form the outer circle and inner horseshoe, are made of very hard sandstone. Each one weighs between 26 and 40 tons and comes from an area about 18 miles north of Stonehenge.

♦ **THE ALTAR STONE**
This faces the Heel Stone, which stands outside the circle, on the avenue leading to it. The altar stone is so placed that it is struck by the rays of the rising sun at the summer solstice.

♦ **STONEHENGE**
Stonehenge is in the English county of Wiltshire, 8 miles north of Salisbury, and is famous for its megalithic (colossal stone) monuments. Some date back over 4,000 years. This area of England is also notable for its round barrows, circular burial mounds of chiefs, dating to about the same period as Stonehenge.

♦ **THE NEOLITHIC AGE**
Whereas earlier prehistoric societies, in the Paleolithic age, had been based on hunting and gathering, Neolithic societies grew their own food and raised livestock.

This revolutionary development began about 12,000 years ago in the Near East, spreading to southeastern and then northeastern Europe around 6000 B.C. The first necropolises (burial sites) appeared between 5000 and 4000 B.C., about the same time as the first farming villages. Huge stones, some carefully decorated, were arranged and covered with mounds, for use as collective tombs.

These chambered tombs may also have served to mark off the territories of different communities. Stonehenge, which is of course not a tomb, seems to have been created to observe the solstices and the phases of the moon. It is extraordinarily sophisticated in its design, and must have involved enormous labor in carving and transporting the hard sarsen stones. Only the surplus wealth and labor and the organizational skills generated by farming made it possible to build such megalithic (from Greek, meaning "large stone") monuments. Farming depended on the cycle of the seasons, and this no doubt accounts for the interest in astronomical observation.

Above: megalithic stones at Palaggiu, Corsica.

♦ **FINDS**
A mysterious find at Stonehenge was the skeleton of a man who had been shot through the chest with a flint arrow, perhaps during a ritual.

BRICKS OF MUD

The Fertile Crescent is the land between the Tigris and the Euphrates Rivers, extending from the Nile Delta to Mesopotamia. Here nomadic hunters and food gatherers settled and became farmers and animal breeders, and this settled existence eventually gave rise to the earliest civilizations. The transformation from villages to the first fortified cities took place in the Near East, between the 10th and 4th millennia B.C. Long before this, natural building materials such as stone and timber had been in use, but from around 9000 B.C. bricks were made. At first these were crude mud bricks, modeled from clay and water and dried in the sun; later the bricks were strengthened by being fired in hearths. In the ancient city-states of Mesopotamia, even the most imposing works, notably the great stepped pyramids, or ziggurats, were built with mud bricks. The sanctuary at the top could be reached by steps and ramps. So, in a land with little natural elevation, it was possible to raise the house of the god or goddess on high and, at the same time, protect it from flooding by the rivers.

♦ FROM VILLAGE TO CITY

About 12,000 years ago, in the Near East, human beings abandoned caves and other natural shelters and started constructing settlements in which to live. The oldest villages were built in areas that were rich in natural resources, so that their inhabitants were able to live by hunting, harvesting foods, and even planned cultivation. Their dwellings were partly sunk into the ground, were circular in plan, and had roofs that were held up with timbers. At the beginning of the 10th millennium B.C., free-standing walls began to be built, dividing interiors into one or more spaces. Unfired clay bricks were used for these, and later houses were built with more complex, rectangular plans. The first fortifications, using walls, ramparts, and ditches, began to appear at about the same time.

The village became, in effect, a city, when it started to serve as a center for storing and distributing produce. This occurred in Mesopotamia during the course of the 4th millennium B.C., when the Sumerians reclaimed the land for agricultural purposes and so accumulated surpluses. The wealth of their increasingly centralized states was amassed in temple complexes which also functioned as administrative centers.

♦ THE ZIGGURAT OF UR-NAMMU

This great tower was built by a Sumerian king and dedicated to the moon god Nanna. Its rectangular base is approximately 148 x 213 feet (45 x 65 m). It stands 66 feet (20 m) high. Its four corners are oriented toward the four cardinal points. Discovered in the 1920s, it has been restored to virtually its original form.

THE SANCTUARY ♦

Standing at the summit of three stepped platforms, this was the house of the god. It was a holy place where the divinity manifested himself to the king and his priests.

THE PROCESSION ♦

Regular offerings, representing the surplus wealth of the community, were carried in procession into the temple complex, where they were checked, weighed, and meticulously recorded by scribes.

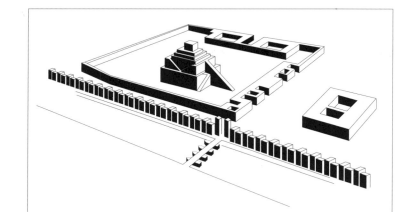

♦ **THE ZIGGURAT'S MEANING**
The ziggurat represented the earth, or perhaps a mountain. Originally the Sumerians may have been a hill people. The ziggurat was believed to be a meeting place for natural and supernatural forces.

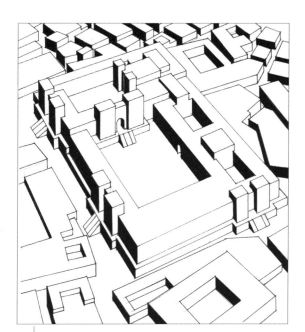

♦ **GROUND PLANS**
In Sumer, ordinary dwellings consisted of rooms around a central courtyard. But temples, palaces, and storehouses were placed around the ziggurat within a large sacred precinct. For security, there was only one entrance to the enclosure within which the ziggurat, and its holy shrine, stood.

♦ **COMMUNITY LIFE**
The first cities were built by people who had realized that there were great advantages in living together in communities. In Mesopotamia cities were isolated, self-sufficient communities: they were not part of larger states, but miniature states in their own right, regarding other cities in the region as rivals.

♦ **BUILDING TECHNIQUES**
Mesopotamia was a region poor in stone. The only available materials were clay, bitumen, and reeds. Reeds were bound together to build huts and other structures. Early mud bricks were formed by hand; later, with the invention of the mold, bricks were made in more regular shapes. Both types of brick were laid out in the sun to dry. Bitumen was used as a cement and as a form of insulation.

♦ **THE ARMED GUARD**
The guard escorted the bearers of offerings right up to the heart of the temple, which in Sumer served also as a treasury and storehouse.

♦ **THE LARGEST ZIGGURAT**
The largest ziggurat must have been the Babylonian one, rebuilt in about 600 B.C. during the reign of Nebuchadnezzar. It may be the edifice referred to in the Bible as the Tower of Babel.

THE PYRAMIDS

The pharaohs who ruled ancient Egypt built on a colossal scale, creating enduring symbols of their power and semidivine status. The pyramids, the Sphinx, and huge temple complexes served to emphasize the link between political and religious authority. Egyptian religion promised an afterlife to its rulers, and later to all its people, and this led the pharaohs to devote enormous resources to the building of tombs where they would spend eternity. The pyramids represent the solution adopted during the Old and Middle Kingdom periods (2686–1795 B.C.). The first pyramids were stepped, like Mesopotamian ziggurats, but then still more imposing structures with smooth triangular sides were built. Later on, pyramids were abandoned in favor of tombs cut into the rocks of the Valley of the Kings, which seemed to offer greater security for the pharaohs' mummified bodies and the treasures buried with them. The pyramids themselves have defied the passage of time, thanks to their monumental solidity. As an Arab proverb puts it, "Time challenges all things, but the pyramids challenge time."

♦ INSIDE THE COLOSSUS
At the center of the pyramid was the funerary chamber. This was where the great stone sarcophagus was placed, which held the pharaoh's mummified body. The chamber could only be reached through a maze of galleries, designed to prevent thieves from violating the tomb and looting its treasures.

♦ BUILDING THE PYRAMIDS
To complete a pyramid, the ancient Egyptians raised great stone blocks higher and higher until the apex was reached. Scholars still argue about how this was achieved.

THE THIRD PYRAMID ♦
The pharaoh Mycerinus (2532–2503 B.C.) ordered the building of the third and last of the famous pyramids at Giza. It is the smallest of the group, 230 feet (70 m) high and 345 feet (105 m) along each side.

THE STONE BLOCKS ♦
Stone blocks from limestone quarries on the other side of the Nile were transported by boat. Then they were put on wooden sleds, which were pulled along specially built ramps made of crushed stone. Once the undertaking was completed, the ramps were dismantled.

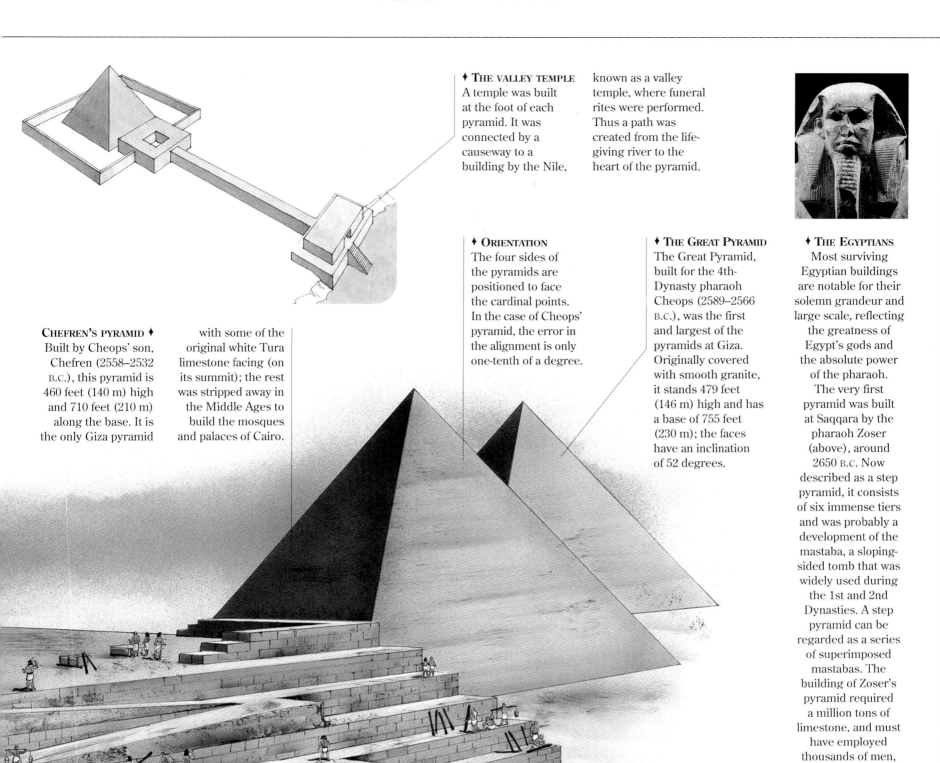

♦ **THE VALLEY TEMPLE**
A temple was built at the foot of each pyramid. It was connected by a causeway to a building by the Nile, known as a valley temple, where funeral rites were performed. Thus a path was created from the life-giving river to the heart of the pyramid.

♦ **ORIENTATION**
The four sides of the pyramids are positioned to face the cardinal points. In the case of Cheops' pyramid, the error in the alignment is only one-tenth of a degree.

♦ **THE GREAT PYRAMID**
The Great Pyramid, built for the 4th-Dynasty pharaoh Cheops (2589–2566 B.C.), was the first and largest of the pyramids at Giza. Originally covered with smooth granite, it stands 479 feet (146 m) high and has a base of 755 feet (230 m); the faces have an inclination of 52 degrees.

♦ **THE EGYPTIANS**
Most surviving Egyptian buildings are notable for their solemn grandeur and large scale, reflecting the greatness of Egypt's gods and the absolute power of the pharaoh.
The very first pyramid was built at Saqqara by the pharaoh Zoser (above), around 2650 B.C. Now described as a step pyramid, it consists of six immense tiers and was probably a development of the mastaba, a sloping-sided tomb that was widely used during the 1st and 2nd Dynasties. A step pyramid can be regarded as a series of superimposed mastabas. The building of Zoser's pyramid required a million tons of limestone, and must have employed thousands of men, who are believed to have been recruited from distant villages. It has been suggested that the enormous collective effort involved in building the first pyramid served to bind together the peoples of a land that had only been unified in relatively recent times. Legend names the architect responsible for it as Imhotep, Zoser's chief minister, who was eventually worshiped as a god. Forty-seven pyramids are currently known. They are spread over a vast territory, including Nubia in the distant south, but all are sited to the west of the course of the Nile.

CHEFREN'S PYRAMID ♦
Built by Cheops' son, Chefren (2558–2532 B.C.), this pyramid is 460 feet (140 m) high and 710 feet (210 m) along the base. It is the only Giza pyramid with some of the original white Tura limestone facing (on its summit); the rest was stripped away in the Middle Ages to build the mosques and palaces of Cairo.

♦ **THE WORKFORCE**
A few skilled workers – stone-cutters, sculptors, and bricklayers – were employed on monuments all year round. The main labor force consisted of farmers who were recruited for the four months during which the flooding of the Nile brought work in the fields to a standstill.

♦ **THE NECROPOLIS OF GIZA**
This enormous funerary complex stands near Cairo, not far from the Nile. The monuments include the Great Sphinx and the three large pyramids of Cheops, Chefren, and Mycerinus.

THE TEMPLE

The art and architecture of ancient Greece have for centuries been regarded as models of harmony and proportion. The Greeks devoted most of their architectural efforts to building temples, the beauty of which was a matter of civic pride as well as an expression of religious devotion. For much of its history, ancient Greece was divided into small city-states, and each city-state, or polis, had at least one temple of its own, just as centuries later every town in Europe had its own church. The most famous of all Greek temples is the Parthenon in Athens, built on the Acropolis, the citadel overlooking the city; it represented the culmination of centuries of architectural experience. The Greek temple was the home of one or more gods, not a place for worshipers to gather in. It was surrounded by a temple precinct, the *temenos*, containing buildings and sculptures; its perimeter followed the lay of the land, in harmony with the natural surroundings.

♦ **PERICLES' ATHENS**
The world of the Greek city-states was very different from that of the earlier ancient civilizations of the Mediterranean and the Near East. Some city-states, notably Athens, were democracies in which all male citizens (but not slaves) could take part in government. Even city-states that were not democracies gave greater rights to their citizens than was usual elsewhere. Instead of sumptuous palaces or colossal tombs, the most important buildings were devoted to civic and religious purposes, and the arts employed in making them entered into the daily lives of the people. Athens was the main power in Greece in the 5th century, when the polis reached its zenith. The city-states fought against one another, siding with either Athens or its great rival, Sparta; but they also proved capable of joining forces to defeat the Persian empire. When this conflict was over (449 B.C.), the Athenian leader, Pericles (above), who was in power from 461 to 429 B.C., proposed to glorify the city and harness the skills of his fellow citizens by rebuilding the Acropolis, which the Persians had burned down. In Athens this was a period of extraordinary energy, and in a few years it proved possible to renovate the entire Acropolis, putting up the Parthenon and other famous buildings.

♦ **THE STATUE OF ATHENA PARTHENOS**
Created by Phidias, entirely from gold, ivory, and precious stones, this colossal statue was about 40 feet (12 m) high and stood in a sanctuary inside the temple. At first it was much criticized because Phidias had shown himself and Pericles on the goddess's shield.

THE PROPYLAEA ♦
This is the term used for the gateway to a temple precinct. For the propylaea on the Athenian Acropolis, the architect Mnesicles erected a building which followed the sloping ground. Crossing it, the visitor sees how the arrangement of the Parthenon and the other buildings sets each one off to advantage.

♦ COLUMNS AND CAPITALS

These main features of the Greek temple are divided into three orders. The Doric Order is the earliest and plainest: the columns have no base and shallow fluting (vertical grooves); they support an undecorated architrave and a frieze. The Ionic Order is slender and more decorated: the capital carries scroll-like volutes; the columns have pedestal bases and deeper fluting, and support a three-band architrave and a frieze. In the later Corinthian Order, which is even more slender, the capital is inspired by plant forms. The Greeks adopted it almost exclusively for interiors, but the Romans later used it more widely.

THE WEST PEDIMENT ♦

The sculptures show a fight between Athena and Poseidon, the sea god, for possession of Attica, the region of which Athens was the center. All the deities and heroes of the region take part.

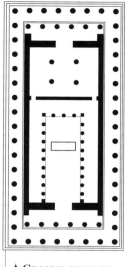

♦ GROUND PLAN OF THE PARTHENON

The simplest and oldest Greek temples have a rectangular chamber with a porch, or *stoa*, in front of it. The more complex temples have a hall surrounded by columns. An intermediate solution was a temple with columns on each of the short sides.

♦ THE COLONNADE

This is built with an acute understanding of optical effects. The vertical elements lean inward and upward to correct the optical effect of falling forward. The corner columns are a little thicker than the others since they are seen against the sky and would otherwise appear thinner than those which have the walls as a background. The architraves and cornices are slightly convex, in order not to look curved in the middle.

♦ PHIDIAS AND THE ARCHITECTS OF THE ACROPOLIS

Two architects, Ictinus and Callicrates, were commissioned to design the temple. But Pericles appointed Phidias, a famous Athenian sculptor, goldsmith, and painter, to direct the building work. Phidias therefore supervised, and probably participated in, the decoration of the Parthenon with mythological and battle scenes. The most celebrated of these is the large marble frieze depicting the solemn procession in honor of Athena. The Parthenon offers a great variety of splendid visual effects in the dazzling Greek light. It can be viewed from many angles, from the city or from inside the sacred enclosure, and it also looks different at different times of day, depending on the interplay of light and shadow. In antiquity it would have had a much more vivid appearance, since it was painted in a number of colors; in fact, the Greek temple can be regarded as having been a huge painted sculpture. The reliefs, and other decorative features of the temple, were carved in the workshops, and the columned sections and other elements were very carefully cut to join up perfectly; only when this had been done were the stones put in place. Above: part of the frieze.

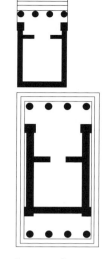

♦ THE PROCESSION

At the end of each July, during the festival known as the Panathenaea, a procession left the city for the Acropolis. It carried an embroidered cloth which was draped over the statue of Athena Parthenos (Athena the Virgin), patron and protector of Athens. The frieze around the inner part of the Parthenon, 3 feet (1 m) high and 525 feet (160 m) long, shows citizens of various types playing their parts in the procession.

THE THEATER

The ancient Greeks invented the drama and built the first theaters. These were in the open air, and were so constructed that they were extremely functional but also harmonized with the landscape. At first, the Greeks made use of natural, semicircular slopes where the audience sat, looking down on a flat space where the performance took place; "theatron" in fact designates the place occupied by the spectators. Then, probably from the 6th century B.C., wooden seats were installed, which were supported by scaffolding. Performances were attended by the entire population, and this made it necessary to build theaters with tiers of stone seats, capable of holding more people and safe from the risk of collapse. The Greek theater, which was later copied and modified by the Romans, is still a model of simple and effective building.

♦ GREEK AND ROMAN THEATERS
The ruins of Greek theaters can be found from Sicily to Turkey. The eastern and southern coasts of the Mediterranean are dotted with the remains of theaters built by the Romans, or adapted by them from theaters that were originally Greek.

Rome's first important theater was erected by Pompey in the year 55 B.C. Although semicircular like Greek theaters, it stood on flat terrain; this could be done because new building techniques enabled the Romans to raise multiple tiers in the absence of a natural slope. The Roman theater was usually found in the city and not on its outskirts, as was normally the case with Greek theaters.

In the imperial period, theaters struggled to compete with the attraction of action entertainments, such as gladiatorial combats and chariot races, which were fast and sometimes fatally dangerous. These drew huge crowds and made it necessary to build specialized structures to house them: amphitheaters or circus arenas, at first made with wood and later with brick and stone. Above: the amphitheater at Arles in France, with its typical elliptical form surrounding the central arena in which the performances took place.

♦ THE PERFORMANCE
During the 4th century B.C., when the theater at Delphi was built, the plays most often performed were those written by the great tragic authors, Aeschylus, Sophocles, and Euripides. However, the cultural climate had changed since the time of those authors; the brief heyday of Athenian democracy, when theatrical performances were an integral part of civic life, had already passed.

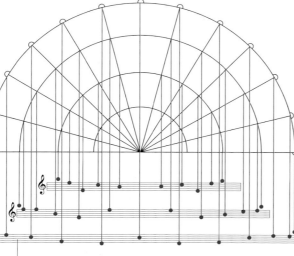

♦ THE THEATER AT EPIDAURUS
This Greek theater is in Argolis, the southeastern region of the Peloponnesus. Said to have been built by Polyclitus the Younger (4th century B.C.), it is still well preserved and has perfect acoustics. It could seat up to 15,000 spectators on 55 tiers, 21 of which were added during the 2nd century B.C. All the other theaters along the Mediterranean were modified during Roman times.

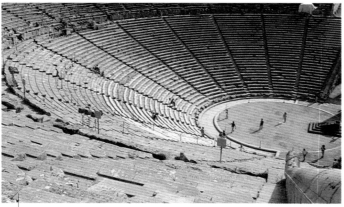

♦ ACOUSTICS
Special building techniques, which are now virtually impossible to trace, amplified the voices of the actors and made it possible to hear any music that was performed in every part of the theater.

THE AUDIENCE ♦
Performances were organized by the authorities and funded by the wealthy. They were put on during public holidays: all other activity came to a halt and the entire population attended; poor people might even be given a token to attend, as reimbursement for a lost day's work.

♦ THE SKENE
This originated as a wooden structure to which the actors could retire to change their masks and costumes. It was later replaced with a stone building which served as an all-purpose stage setting. Depending on the requirements of the drama, the audience was expected to visualize it as a palace, a temple, or any other appropriate background to the action.

♦ THE ORCHESTRA
This was a circular space, about 66 feet (20 m) in diameter, in which the chorus performed. Around 15 individuals made up the chorus, whose dances and chants underscored and commented on the action taking place.

♦ THE CAVEA
The cavea was the semicircle of tiered seats occupied by the spectators. There were two types of seats. Those closest to the skene were for civic dignitaries, patrons, and priests; some seats even had a backrest with an inscription indicating the offices held by the most important people. All other seats were for the free population: only slaves were excluded.

ROMAN EMPIRE

In the 2nd and 3rd centuries A.D., Rome was the capital of an empire that stretched from southern Scotland to the Persian Gulf. One purpose of Roman architecture was to express the might of this empire. Palaces, baths, temples, bridges, and aqueducts were proof of the wealth, skills, and resources at the command of the state. In addition, the rapidly growing urban population was provided with grand public entertainments: games, races, and exhibitions, for which monumental buildings such as amphitheaters and circuses were constructed. Military parades were also spectacular, and every emperor glorified himself and his reign by ordering the erection of a triumphal arch, through which troops passed on their return from a successful expedition.

♦ **TRIUMPHAL ARCH**
The Roman Senate had an arch built next to the Colosseum, in Constantine's honor. In A.D. 316 the emperor arrived in Rome with his army and prisoners of war to celebrate the tenth anniversary of his rise to power.

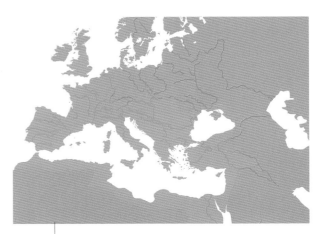

♦ **THE ROMAN EMPIRE**
Under Trajan (A.D. 98–117), the Roman Empire reached its greatest extent, taking in the entire Mediterranean basin and large areas of western Europe including present-day France and southern Britain.

THE COLOSSEUM ♦
The biggest permanent amphi-theater in Rome was ordered by Vespasian and inaugurated by Titus in A.D. 80. The Colosseum could hold up to 50,000 spectators for the gladiatorial contests, animal hunts, and other (usually bloody and destructive) games staged there. The shows were provided mainly by people wishing to ingratiate themselves with the populace, such as office-holders or candidates for office.

THE ARMY AND ♦
THE PEOPLE
Early in the 4th century A.D., Rome experienced a population explosion, which brought with it a building boom. This was made possible by the peace and good order imposed by Constantine, the first Christian emperor. Here the army, composed of professional soldiers from various parts of the empire, marches through the city in a show of strength; by this time it had often shown itself capable of making or breaking emperors.

THE IMPERIAL FORA ♦
The low ground between the Palatine, Capitoline, and Esquiline Hills was reclaimed in the 6th century B.C. A market (forum) was opened, after which the area became the center of public and religious life. When the republic became an empire, the fora were enlarged along lines laid down by Julius Caesar. Among the buildings erected were a new curia (where the senators met), a new basilica (where public meetings were held and justice was administered), a Greek and a Latin library, and a market on several levels.

RECYCLED MATERIALS ♦
To build the Arch of Constantine, many items were removed from earlier monuments and skillfully combined to create a homogeneous whole. The symbols on the arch helped to spread new concepts – of a rigidly hierarchical and bureaucratic society – which characterized the late empire.

♦ TRAJAN'S COLUMN
Compared with earlier columns supporting statues of great Romans, Trajan's Column was highly original. This was because of the way it was decorated, in a continuous spiral relief comprising a narrative of the two Dacian wars won by Trajan in A.D. 102–6. An allegorical figure of Victory separates the narratives of the two campaigns. The scenes of battle and capitulation have provided historians with otherwise unavailable information. Rome's enemies are shown as recognizable human beings. Also, the colonization of Dacia (present-day Romania) is shown, as if in a huge history carved in stone. Between c. 176 and c. 193 a new spiral-decorated column was erected in honor of Marcus Aurelius, and others were later raised in the squares of Constantinople.

♦ THE FRIEZE
Halfway up the monument, above the side arches and along the sides, a continuous bas-relief shows episodes from Constantine's life. Perspective techniques have been used to exalt the figure of the emperor speaking in the forum or distributing rewards after his victory over Maxentius.

ARCHES AND DOMES

The arch was known to the Sumerians and was extensively used by the Etruscans. But the Romans were the first people to exploit its potential to the full. It became the basis for the design of vaults and domes, and these made it possible to cover large, unbroken spaces, and accommodate many people for public business, worship, or recreation. Whereas Greek buildings were essentially rectilinear structures, dedicated to divine rather than human use, the Romans were much more concerned with practical problems of integrated urban architecture. They built on such a large scale that it was desirable to limit the use of stone, which in any case was not easily adapted to covering large spaces. Consequently they made great use of bricks, along with a new material, concrete. This consisted of lime and volcanic dust, mixed with water, which was poured over crushed stone or crumbled bricks, the whole compound setting rock-hard. It could be used to fill the spaces inside brick or stone facings, or to build vaults or domes, as in the case of the Pantheon.

✦ THE PANTHEON

This temple, dedicated to all the gods, was built during the reign of Emperor Augustus. Originally named Octavian, Augustus was the nephew and adopted son of Julius Caesar and became the first Roman emperor after vanquishing all his rivals; he ruled from 27 B.C. to A.D. 14. The Pantheon was rebuilt between A.D. 120 and 125, during the reign of Hadrian, whose admiration for Greek architecture is shown by his use of a portico in the Greek style, attached to a Roman domed structure.

The height of the Pantheon is the same as the diameter of its dome; consequently, a sphere could be fitted into the inner space, which perhaps represents the cosmos. The spectacular dome was the largest example of its kind in the world, right down to the 20th century. When Christianity became the religion of the empire, pagan temples were shunned, and up to the 7th century many were dismantled and used to build churches. But in 609 Pope Boniface IV consecrated the Pantheon and ordered quantities of bones of Christian martyrs to be removed from the Catacombs and deposited in the new church. This was renamed Our Lady and all the Martyrs. The Pantheon now holds the remains of Raphael and other famous artists and of the kings of Italy.

✦ FROM PAGAN TEMPLE TO CHRISTIAN CHURCH

In A.D. 609, a year after he had received the Pantheon as a gift from the Byzantine emperor Phocas, Pope Boniface IV led a procession into the building, which had not been in use for over a century. The pope proceeded to consecrate the building and it became a church dedicated to early Christian martyrs, whose relics were transferred to the site.

✦ THE OCULUS

Light enters the interior through the eye, or oculus, of the dome. An opening at the summit, with a diameter of some 30 feet (9 m), the oculus symbolized the sun and served to cast light on to the statues of gods and goddesses, which were placed in deep niches in the circular wall. The wall itself was about 23 feet (7 m) thick.

THE DOME ✦

The "honeycomb" pattern of hollows on the inside of the dome (known as coffering) was made by wooden "casts" within the concrete. Once they were removed, the coffering was revealed. It accentuated the perspective and made the dome lighter.

PAGAN STATUES ✦

Pagan statues stood in niches in the interior of the Pantheon, but were removed before the pope entered. They were replaced with Christian relics and images.

THE PORTICO ✦

The inscription on the triangular pediment above the entrance portico records the fact that the consul Marcus Agrippa built the temple – but actually the present Pantheon was rebuilt by Hadrian, who modestly kept the dedication to his predecessor. Sixteen Corinthian columns surround the portico.

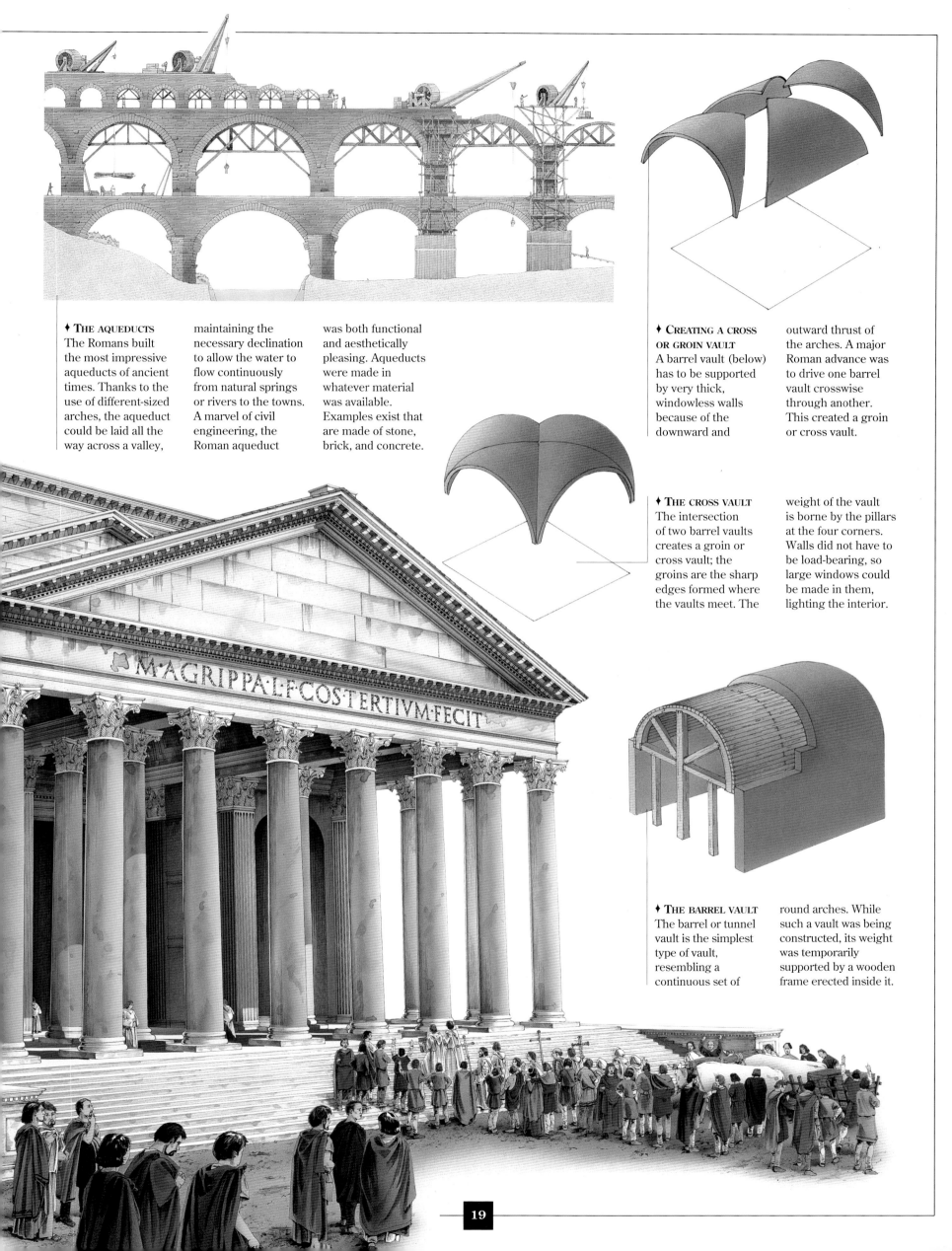

✦ THE AQUEDUCTS
The Romans built the most impressive aqueducts of ancient times. Thanks to the use of different-sized arches, the aqueduct could be laid all the way across a valley, maintaining the necessary declination to allow the water to flow continuously from natural springs or rivers to the towns. A marvel of civil engineering, the Roman aqueduct was both functional and aesthetically pleasing. Aqueducts were made in whatever material was available. Examples exist that are made of stone, brick, and concrete.

✦ CREATING A CROSS OR GROIN VAULT
A barrel vault (below) has to be supported by very thick, windowless walls because of the downward and outward thrust of the arches. A major Roman advance was to drive one barrel vault crosswise through another. This created a groin or cross vault.

✦ THE CROSS VAULT
The intersection of two barrel vaults creates a groin or cross vault; the groins are the sharp edges formed where the vaults meet. The weight of the vault is borne by the pillars at the four corners. Walls did not have to be load-bearing, so large windows could be made in them, lighting the interior.

✦ THE BARREL VAULT
The barrel or tunnel vault is the simplest type of vault, resembling a continuous set of round arches. While such a vault was being constructed, its weight was temporarily supported by a wooden frame erected inside it.

THE BASILICA

With the Edict of Milan in A.D. 313, the Emperor Constantine ended the persecution of Christianity, which rapidly became the dominant, and then the sole, religion of the Roman Empire. From this time the Church took over existing buildings and arranged for the construction of new ones for worship. The model chosen for Christian churches was not the pagan temple, a place set aside for effigies of the gods and priestly ceremonies, but the basilica, a hall which served the Romans as a covered market and courthouse. The ground plan of this building was a rectangle, divided by columns into a nave and two aisles. The sloping roof was made of wooden beams. A different type of church design, more common in the Eastern Empire, had a central plan, covered by one or two domes. The basilican and central-plan types were synthesized in the church of Santa Sophia at Constantinople.

♦ **CONSTANTINOPLE**
In A.D. 330 Constantinople (ancient Byzantium, modern Istanbul) became the capital of the Roman Empire in the East. Unlike the Western Empire, the East survived the 5th-century barbarian invasions and Constantinople remained the greatest city in Christendom almost until its capture by the Ottoman Turks in 1453. Developing away from its Roman heritage, the state of which Constantinople was the capital became the Greek-Christian Byzantine Empire. Byzantine philosophy mingled Christian with earlier Greek concepts, and Byzantine art and architecture also had a mixed cultural heritage – Greek, Roman, and Oriental. The church of Santa Sophia represents a fusion of these elements. Technically, it marks an advance in the elegant, accurate placing of a dome on a square base. The mosaics were designed to reflect the light, which is diffused from many sources, including the windows at the base of the dome; the ever-changing effect creates a transcendent atmosphere. The Emperor Justinian (527–65) summoned artists from all over the Greco-Roman world to build and decorate the church. The work was supervised by Isidore of Miletus and a great mathematician and engineer, Anthemius of Tralles. Above: Istanbul today.

THE DESIGN ♦
The main area of the church has an almost square ground plan; on it stand the slightly flattened dome and two half-domes at the sides, which buttress it. The windows at the base of the dome and in many other places fill the church with light.

♦ **SANTA SOPHIA**
The church was built on the site of an older building, destroyed during the Nika Riots of 532.

When Constantinople finally fell to the Turks in 1453, they converted it into a mosque, adding four minarets.

♦ **THE BASILICA OF MAXENTIUS**
Built in Rome during the early 4th century B.C., this is one of the few pre-Christian basilicas of which there are substantial remains. Its surviving vaults are impressive.

♦ Light

Forty windows at the base of the dome let in a diffused light which displays to wonderful effect the mosaics, the traceried capitals, the vari-colored marbles, the red and blue of the porphyry, and the other colored stones.

♦ San Vitale

In Byzantine churches, Roman building techniques were combined with a wealth of Greco-Oriental decoration. A magnificent example is San Vitale in Ravenna, Italy, which was built by Justinian and consecrated in 547. Its octagonal ground plan and dome became models for later buildings, in both the West and the East, and its mosaics are world-famous.

♦ The mosaics

Small cubes of colored marble, stone, or glass were mounted side by side on a stone surface, making up a picture or decoration; this art is known as mosaic. Gold and silver were also used in the mosaics of Santa Sophia. They were set in unevenly so that they would be certain to catch the light. There is an early Christian example of this art (below) in the Mausoleum of Galla Placidia in Ravenna, from the mid-5th century.

♦ The central plan

Central-plan buildings give a more contained sense of space than the rectangular-plan basilican model. The cross shape represents the crucifixion; the dome represents heaven, often with a mosaic or painting of Christ as Judge looking down on the congregation.

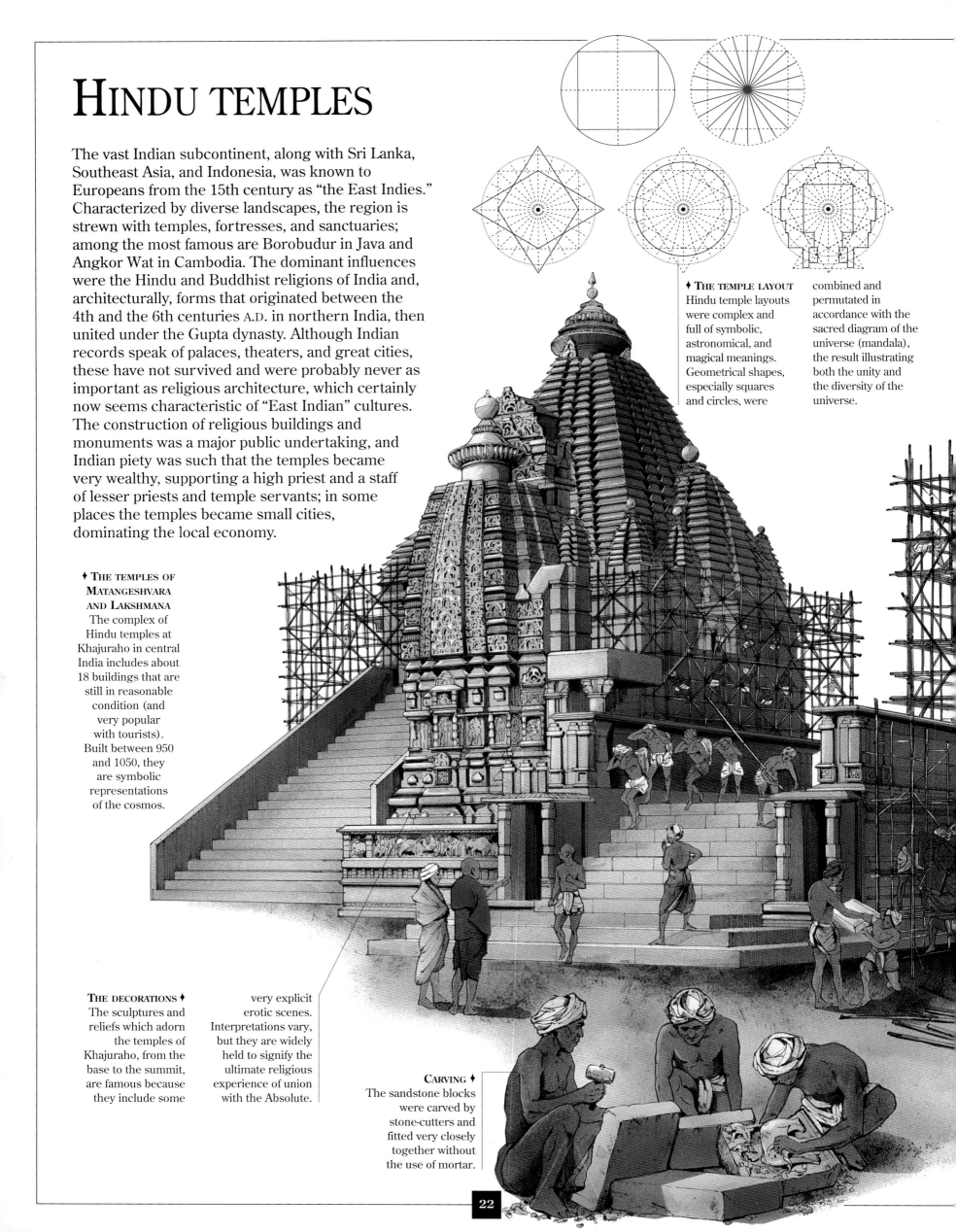

HINDU TEMPLES

The vast Indian subcontinent, along with Sri Lanka, Southeast Asia, and Indonesia, was known to Europeans from the 15th century as "the East Indies." Characterized by diverse landscapes, the region is strewn with temples, fortresses, and sanctuaries; among the most famous are Borobudur in Java and Angkor Wat in Cambodia. The dominant influences were the Hindu and Buddhist religions of India and, architecturally, forms that originated between the 4th and the 6th centuries A.D. in northern India, then united under the Gupta dynasty. Although Indian records speak of palaces, theaters, and great cities, these have not survived and were probably never as important as religious architecture, which certainly now seems characteristic of "East Indian" cultures. The construction of religious buildings and monuments was a major public undertaking, and Indian piety was such that the temples became very wealthy, supporting a high priest and a staff of lesser priests and temple servants; in some places the temples became small cities, dominating the local economy.

♦ **THE TEMPLE LAYOUT**
Hindu temple layouts were complex and full of symbolic, astronomical, and magical meanings. Geometrical shapes, especially squares and circles, were combined and permutated in accordance with the sacred diagram of the universe (mandala), the result illustrating both the unity and the diversity of the universe.

♦ **THE TEMPLES OF MATANGESHVARA AND LAKSHMANA**
The complex of Hindu temples at Khajuraho in central India includes about 18 buildings that are still in reasonable condition (and very popular with tourists). Built between 950 and 1050, they are symbolic representations of the cosmos.

THE DECORATIONS ♦
The sculptures and reliefs which adorn the temples of Khajuraho, from the base to the summit, are famous because they include some very explicit erotic scenes. Interpretations vary, but they are widely held to signify the ultimate religious experience of union with the Absolute.

CARVING ♦
The sandstone blocks were carved by stone-cutters and fitted very closely together without the use of mortar.

A TAPERING TOWER ✦
The shape of the tower was probably suggested by the appearance of ancient bamboo coverings. The size of the horizontal and vertical elements was progressively reduced so that the tower became narrower as it rose, enhancing the sense of upward ascent.

✦ THE HEART OF THE TEMPLE
At the center of the temple was a small, unadorned cell with only one entrance; here was kept the image of the deity to whom the temple was dedicated. From the cell, a vestibule led to a large main hall where worshipers gathered, and beyond that was the portico. The temple of Lakshmana was dedicated to Vishnu, its companion (on the left) to Shiva.

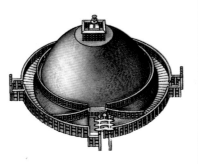

✦ THE EVOLUTION OF ARCHITECTURAL STYLES
For much of the history of the subcontinent, India's architecture was primarily religious, originating with Hindu and Buddhist temples and with stupas (above) – dome-shaped Buddhist shrines which housed relics and were decorated with episodes from the life of the Buddha (5th century B.C.). The great age of temple building began in the 4th century A.D. Although the construction and decoration varied in detail between regions, all the temples were characterized by an oblong structure built around a central cell with a tower rising above it. From the 7th century this style was elaborated; plans became more complex, and tower forms proliferated. They were covered with countless superbly carved figures, reliefs, cornices, and pinnacles. In fact, here and in many other parts of Asia, architecture was treated as subordinate to decoration, which was often so profuse that it obscured any sense of structure.

✦ THE BUILDING YARD
Priests supervised every phase of temple building; this was partly a spiritual task, since they took responsibility for the achievement of harmony between the works of man and the cosmos, the human and the divine. Ancient Indian texts served as manuals for the architects, providing them with technical as well as spiritual direction. The people who built Indian temples almost always remained anonymous, but it is known that they were organized into guilds of itinerant craftsmen.

THE MOSQUE

For all Islamic peoples, the center of religious and public life is the mosque, a place of prayer that is also a meeting place, school, and court of justice. Although mosques have been built since the 8th century in a variety of styles, the basic layout has not changed. It consists of a roofed space, lined with columns, that looks out onto a rectangular enclosure. The arrangement is based on the house where early converts to Islam met to be instructed by the Prophet Muhammad. Whatever the orientation of the surrounding buildings and streets, the mosque always faces in the direction of the Ka'aba, a shrine in the holy city of Mecca, to which every Muslim must turn when saying his or her daily prayers. In the mosque, Muslims pray to Allah without the mediation of priests or holy images.

✦ ISLAM
From the 7th century a new force burst upon the world. In Arabia the Prophet Muhammad proclaimed the might and majesty of Allah, and the teachings of this monotheistic religion were recorded in a holy book, the Qur'an. After some years of persecution, the Prophet Muhammad enjoyed increasing success in converting the Arabs, who broke out of the Arabian peninsula in an extraordinary explosion of military and religious zeal. Between the 8th and 10th centuries, conquests and conversions spread the new religion over a vast area, from the Atlantic to central Asia; later it would reach Nigeria and Indonesia.
Islam was opposed to the worship of idols, and consequently Muslims developed a special appreciation of abstract decoration. Since the Arabs were in origin a nomadic people, they lacked an architectural tradition, basing their building on a creative development of ancient Greek, Persian, and Christian styles. Above: the mosque at Kairouan, Tunisia.

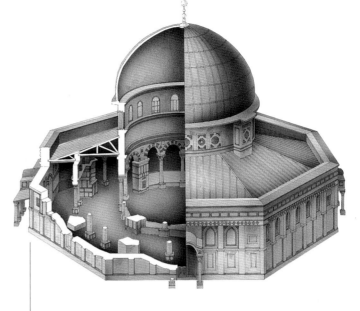

✦ THE DOME OF THE ROCK
Built in about A.D. 690 on the Temple Mount in Jerusalem, the Dome of the Rock is the second most holy place in Islam. It has an octagonal ground plan derived from Roman and Christian models such as the 4th-century Church of the Resurrection, also in Jerusalem. Two concentric corridors enable people to walk around the rock, from which the Prophet Muhammad is believed to have ascended to heaven on a miraculous "Night Journey."

✦ BADSHAHI
One of the largest mosques in the East, Badshahi stands in the ancient city of Lahore, Pakistan. Its courtyard is bigger than, for example, St. Mark's Square in Venice, and it can hold as many as a million pilgrims.

THE COURTYARD ✦
Roofed arcades run around a courtyard in which stands the fountain for ablutions. In hot, dry countries where water was often in short supply, the fountains of mosques in small towns were also pressed into service as the main water supply.

♦ **THE ALHAMBRA PALACE IN GRANADA**
The Arabs invaded and settled the south of Spain during the second half of the 8th century; their final stronghold there fell only in 1492. The Alhambra ("Red House") is a sumptuous residential complex built in various stages from the mid-13th century. It lies in a secluded spot on a green hill, comprises a succession of pavilions, courtyards, and gardens, and is surrounded by walls and 24 towers of red brick. The heart of the building is the Court of the Lions, filled with wonderful decorations, elaborate inscriptions, and sparkling water.

♦ **THE PORCH**
The huge porch rises far above the roof-line of the building.

♦ **THE DOME**
Beneath this bulbous dome is a wall facing Mecca, in front of which the worshipers pray; it is indicated by a richly ornamented niche called the "qibla." Near it is a pulpit from which the imam speaks.

♦ **THE MINARETS**
The domed towers are the minarets, from which the muezzins summon worshipers to prayer five times a day.

♦ **THE MINARET OF THE GREAT MOSQUE AT ALEPPO**
Built in 1092, this stone tower stands on a square base and is five stories and 148 feet (45 m) high. At its top is an open veranda from which the muezzin calls Muslims to prayer. Often the job of the muezzin is hereditary. Minarets vary in form, depending on the architectural traditions of the country in which they are built. The most common type of minaret is tall, cylindrical, and built of brick.

♦ **CROWDS AT PRAYER**
As they pray, Muslims follow a series of rhythmic movements. The entire congregation faces in the direction of the Ka'aba, the most holy shrine of Islam, which stands in the center of the Grand Mosque in Mecca. Worshipers for whom there is no room inside the mosque stay outside in the courtyard. The men pray in the sun while the women, wrapped in their pale veils, are in the shade on the left.

CHRISTIANITY IN THE WEST

With the decline of the Roman Empire in the West, most of Europe was overrun by barbarian peoples and many skills were lost. But Christianity survived, and gradually a new order arose, based on feudal lordship and a powerful Church. Great stone buildings were erected that dominated the low wooden houses of the common people. Imposing churches and abbeys, with high bell towers that were visible from a great distance, served as landmarks for the pilgrims who journeyed from shrine to shrine. The first great medieval European style was the Romanesque, characterized by round arches, very thick walls, and massive pillars. The result, in churches and cathedrals, is monumental and austere. Building Romanesque and later cathedrals took decades or generations, and involved the whole community. Itinerant craftsmen traveled from one building site to another, bringing word of distant lands. The people, used to small dwellings, were gathered into a building of overwhelming size. There, even if they were illiterate, they could "read" narratives about Christ and the saints, Good and Evil, in painted or carved images.

◆ **ROMANESQUE ARCHITECTURE**
During what came to be known as the "Dark Ages" (the centuries following the fall of the Roman Empire, down to about A.D. 1000), people did in fact make some important advances in building techniques. Resources and skills were devoted above all to the building of churches and cathedrals. A prime example is Durham Cathedral in northern England; the illustration shows how the cathedral dominated the small city and the surrounding countryside.

DURHAM CATHEDRAL ◆
Building started in 1093 and was complete by about 1130. The west front has two towers, and there is a large square tower over the transept (the "arms" of a cross-shaped church). The walls are thick and the pillars massive. The aisles are elongated, following a model seen most widely in France, but also in central and southern Europe.

◆ **THE ROOF**
The problem of how to cover large areas with stone vaulting was solved in a few decades, between 980 and 1020. The stability of the vaults over the largest space, the nave, affected the entire structure. The addition of side aisles enabled the weight to be distributed over a larger area.

Durham Cathedral is the first structure in which ribs are used to take the main thrust of the vaults, discharging the weight of the roof at points where there were massive columns to take it. The aisles are composed of a number of bays, each divided by the ribs into four segments.

◆ **SCULPTURE**
Early Christians condemned images and effigies; but by about A.D. 1000 the Church had come to recognize their value as a means of communication. Sculptures were a way of showing the Church's teaching in pictures that people would understand. The stone portals surrounding Romanesque doors were filled with vivid, vigorously carved scenes of human salvation and damnation. Inside the church too, the worshipers were surrounded by images illustrating episodes from the Bible. Left: a figure of Christ above the door of Autun Cathedral, France.

THE GROUND PLAN ♦
The Romanesque style established the Latin-cross ground plan as the norm for Western churches. The interior was divided along its length into three areas – the nave and flanking aisles – and crossed by the transept, between the nave and the chancel.

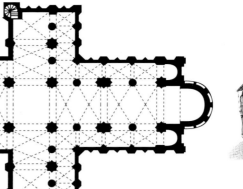

♦ ABBEYS
After the fall of the Roman Empire in the West, there was no single political authority. Germanic and other peoples burst into western and southern Europe, while the expanding culture of Islam sought to dominate the Mediterranean. Trade routes were disrupted and a fragmented Europe was made up of increasingly self-sufficient societies. From the 9th century there was a degree of political and cultural revival under Charlemagne and his successors (the Carolingian dynasty). The process was carried forward mainly by the monastic orders, beginning with the Benedictines. They established networks of effectively independent abbeys or monasteries where learning was cultivated; in particular, the monks preserved and copied or translated ancient texts. The abbey and its estates formed a self-sufficient unit, including the houses of craftsmen and peasants, barns, mills, and facilities for storing grain. Abbeys gave hospitality to pilgrims traveling to Rome or Santiago de Compostela, the most visited holy places. Until well into the Middle Ages, abbeys rather than towns were the real economic and cultural, as well as religious, centers. The most important was Cluny (above), whose rebuilt abbey church (1088–1130) was the largest of the Middle Ages.

♦ GRANDEUR
The grandeur of Durham Cathedral and its monumental presence are enhanced by its position, surrounded by small, low houses, on a hill. The site is unwalled, since adequate protection is offered by the loop of the river.

♦ MOVES FORWARD
Durham Cathedral is an exceptional building in England, where timber-framing was usual and vaulted ceilings became common only later on, in the Gothic period. The cathedral is also remarkable in that the nave contains embryonic flying buttresses. These were features that anticipated much later solutions to structural problems.

TRIUMPH OF THE CHURCH

The Romanesque-style church exuded solidity and strength; like a fortress, it provided worshipers with a refuge from evil. But by the mid-12th century the triumph of Christianity in Europe had prepared the way for a change of emphasis, to soaring, joyful emotion and the promise of heavenly light. These were expressed by a new architectural style, Gothic, made possible by crucial technical innovations and the growing wealth of the cities, which funded the building of great cathedrals. Gothic was technically the most advanced building style of the Middle Ages and is often seen as the culmination of the "Age of Faith." Gothic cathedrals could be raised to far greater heights than their predecessors, thanks to engineering discoveries which meant that monumental stone structures no longer needed the support of thick load-bearing walls. And this, in turn, meant that large window openings could be left in the walls and filled with stained glass, lighting the interior with a blaze of color.

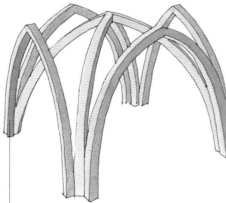

✦ RIBS
Gothic vaults were supported by a framework of stone ribs which carried the weight down the pillars to the floor. The earliest were quadripartite, with each bay divided into four compartments by diagonal ribs. Later on, sexpartite ribs and other arrangements were used.

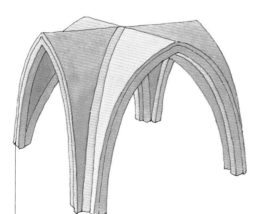

✦ POINTED ARCHES
With pointed arches, a cross vault can be built not only with a square base (as in the case of two intersecting barrel vaults) but even with a rectangular or irregular base. This is because pointed arches can be designed with different diameters to reach the same height. This was known and exploited by Islamic architects from the 7th century.

STAINED-GLASS ✦ WINDOWS
The windows, including the spectacular rose window on the façade, consist of pieces of colored glass, assembled to form a picture and held together by a lead frame. Light falling on the window lights up the picture and flings bright colors into the interior.

✦ CHARTRES
By the 12th century, feudal Europe had attained a degree of political stability and there was considerable economic growth. The great Gothic cathedrals first appeared in the Ile de France, the area around Paris. They were expressions of community pride, and cities competed with one another to erect taller and more beautiful buildings. The first stones of Chartres Cathedral were laid in 1194.

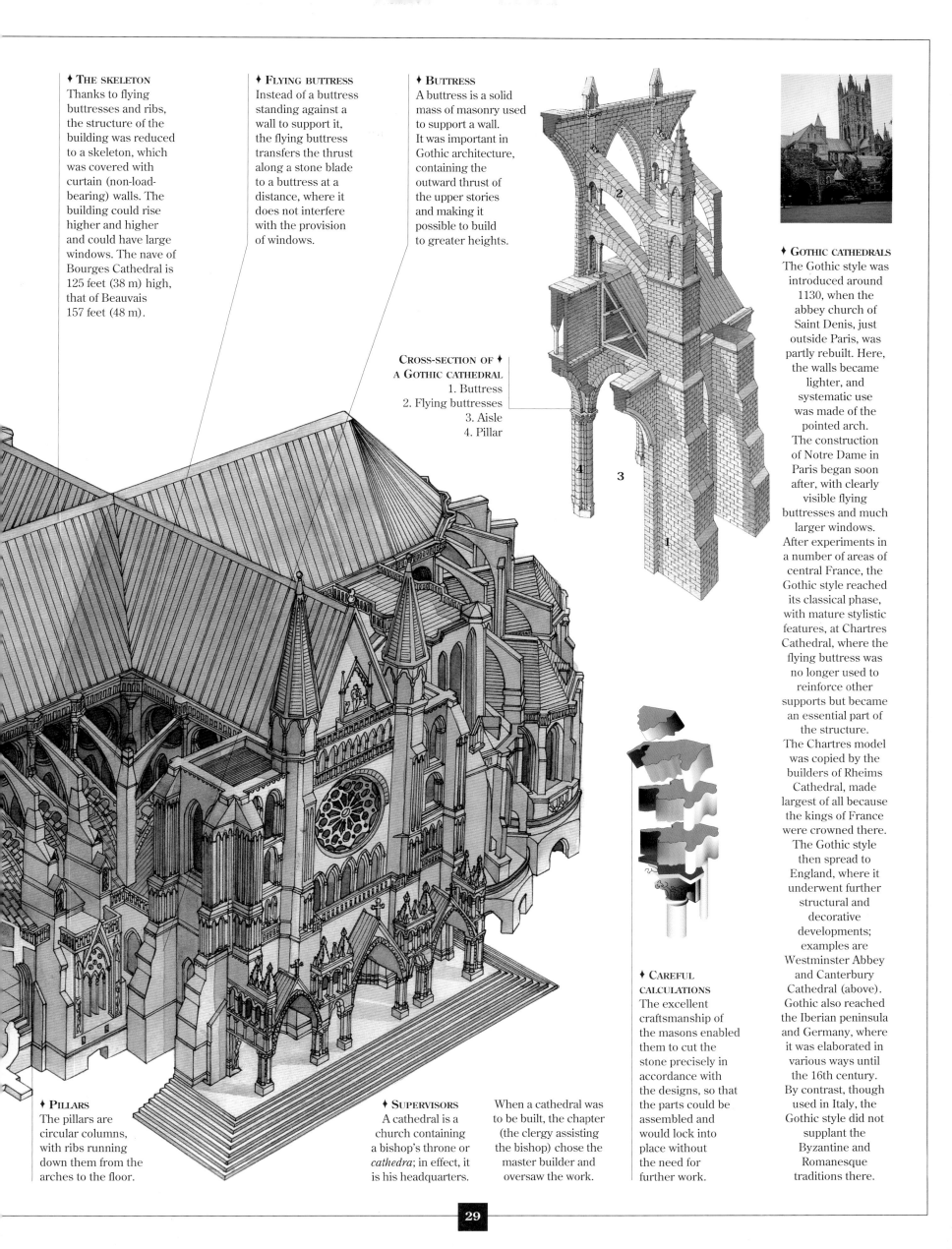

✦ THE SKELETON
Thanks to flying buttresses and ribs, the structure of the building was reduced to a skeleton, which was covered with curtain (non-load-bearing) walls. The building could rise higher and higher and could have large windows. The nave of Bourges Cathedral is 125 feet (38 m) high, that of Beauvais 157 feet (48 m).

✦ FLYING BUTTRESS
Instead of a buttress standing against a wall to support it, the flying buttress transfers the thrust along a stone blade to a buttress at a distance, where it does not interfere with the provision of windows.

✦ BUTTRESS
A buttress is a solid mass of masonry used to support a wall. It was important in Gothic architecture, containing the outward thrust of the upper stories and making it possible to build to greater heights.

CROSS-SECTION OF ✦ A GOTHIC CATHEDRAL
1. Buttress
2. Flying buttresses
3. Aisle
4. Pillar

✦ GOTHIC CATHEDRALS
The Gothic style was introduced around 1130, when the abbey church of Saint Denis, just outside Paris, was partly rebuilt. Here, the walls became lighter, and systematic use was made of the pointed arch. The construction of Notre Dame in Paris began soon after, with clearly visible flying buttresses and much larger windows. After experiments in a number of areas of central France, the Gothic style reached its classical phase, with mature stylistic features, at Chartres Cathedral, where the flying buttress was no longer used to reinforce other supports but became an essential part of the structure. The Chartres model was copied by the builders of Rheims Cathedral, made largest of all because the kings of France were crowned there. The Gothic style then spread to England, where it underwent further structural and decorative developments; examples are Westminster Abbey and Canterbury Cathedral (above). Gothic also reached the Iberian peninsula and Germany, where it was elaborated in various ways until the 16th century. By contrast, though used in Italy, the Gothic style did not supplant the Byzantine and Romanesque traditions there.

✦ CAREFUL CALCULATIONS
The excellent craftsmanship of the masons enabled them to cut the stone precisely in accordance with the designs, so that the parts could be assembled and would lock into place without the need for further work.

✦ PILLARS
The pillars are circular columns, with ribs running down them from the arches to the floor.

✦ SUPERVISORS
A cathedral is a church containing a bishop's throne or *cathedra*; in effect, it is his headquarters.

When a cathedral was to be built, the chapter (the clergy assisting the bishop) chose the master builder and oversaw the work.

DEFENSE

From the 9th and 10th centuries, feudal lords built castles to protect themselves against the Vikings and other barbarian peoples who were still assailing Europe. Initially, these were simple timber stockades consisting of a mound (motte), on which stood a tower, surrounded by a palisade and ditch. Sometimes a second enclosure, the bailey, was linked to the motte, creating the motte-and-bailey castle. From the 10th century, mighty stone towers, or keeps, were built in many places. Later, castles were designed in various combinations of keep, strong gatehouse, and outer defensive wall. Castles were essentially fortified residences in which the feudal nobility could dwell in relative safety, but they also served as the judicial and administrative centers from which the surrounding territory was ruled. Houses huddled around the castle, becoming villages and even towns. Cities were usually walled for defense, sometimes very formidably. But then the advent of artillery and cannon fire completely changed the kind of fortification required.

♦ STONE SHIELDS
Castles were built all over Europe by medieval lords and monarchs, who might need protection from barbarian raiders, their own populations, or rival lords or monarchs. Strong, high towers made it possible to keep watch on large areas of the surrounding countryside. They also provided a refuge in which the defenders could hope to hold out until relief arrived or the attackers ran out of resources and left. The French king Phillip Augustus (1180–1226) built many castles along the Loire River; these were later transformed into sumptuous residences. English king Edward I (1270–1307) raised a chain of great concentric fortresses to keep the conquered Welsh under control. By the mid-15th century, however, firearms, especially cannon, had become effective weapons of war, and military building changed accordingly. Walls were thicker, in order to resist the shots; inclined, so that cannon balls were more likely to glance off them; and lowered, to make smaller targets. Bastions were designed to thrust out from the angles of the walls into the field; they provided advanced artillery platforms and enabled the defenders to catch any enemy who assaulted the walls in a crossfire. Above: Edlingham Castle, England.

♦ PALMANOVA
In 1593 the Venetian Republic built this fortress city in the Friuli region. Its streets radiate from a hexagonal central square; the thoroughfares reach three of the nine bastions and the three city gates, where the barracks were located. The star-shaped plan, originally found in Renaissance treatises describing ideal cities, was taken over and used for other fortress cities such as Coevorden in the Netherlands.

♦ CARCASSONE
The fortified city of Carcassonne, in southwestern France, is a masterpiece of military architecture. It is protected by concentric walls, which are strengthened by round or semicircular towers at regular intervals.
In 1247, after the Albigensian Crusade, Carcassonne became a French possession.

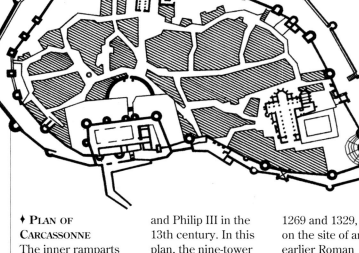

♦ PLAN OF CARCASSONNE
The inner ramparts of Carcassonne were originally constructed by the Visigoths in the 5th century. The outer ramparts were built under Louis IX and Philip III in the 13th century. In this plan, the nine-tower castle is at the bottom left. On the right is the small church of St. Nazaire, which was rebuilt in a late Gothic style between 1269 and 1329, on the site of an earlier Roman church. On the far right is the open-air theater, which was capable of holding an audience of 5,000 people.

♦ **THE DOUBLE RAMPARTS**
The concentric walls were a highly effective means of defense. The outer wall was lower so that the defenders could fire over it at the enemy. If this first wall was stormed, the attackers found themselves exposed to fire from the inner wall.

♦ **THE TOWERS**
The majority of the 52 towers protecting Carcassonne are round and cone-topped. Two large projecting "beaks" protect the Porte Narbonnaise, one of only two gates into the city. The other is the Aude Gate.

THE NEW WORLD

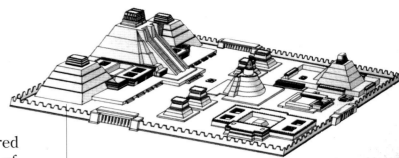

From the 15th century, Europeans, equipped with firearms and able to sail great distances in ocean-going vessels, began to explore and conquer Asia and the Americas. In the New World they encountered and annihilated advanced civilizations such as those of the Mayas and Aztecs in Central America. These peoples built on a monumental scale for religious purposes. Their buildings generally took stepped pyramidal forms, but, unlike the Egyptian pyramids, they rarely contained tombs; they more closely resembled Sumerian ziggurats, having shrines at the top and very steep stairs. In many places these sacred buildings had a new structure built over them every 52 years. According to the ceremonial calendar, this was the length of a cycle, at the end of which the world renewed itself. Astronomy was in fact the most highly developed science among these peoples, and Central American pyramids were probably often used as observatories.

♦ VANISHED CIVILIZATIONS
When Spanish invaders landed in Central America in the mid-16th century, they encountered extremely advanced civilizations.
The oldest was the Mayan civilization in Yucatan, which was already in terminal decline. But to the north, in what is now Mexico, there was a much younger and still vigorous civilization. When the Spanish arrived, it was dominated by the Aztecs, who had built up a great empire by waging war on their neighbors.
In Mayan and Aztec societies, religion was the major unifying force. Mayan and Aztec leaders, like the pharaohs in Egypt, were regarded as gods on earth. They built majestic cities, whose centers were places of worship and symbolic residences of the many deities – one for each element, for each star, and for almost every form of public or private activity. Beyond these ceremonial centers there were planned residential districts with palaces and temples, as well as districts in which each clan or social group had its own piece of land. The cities of the Aztec world had very efficient aqueducts and sewer systems, and were linked by a network of roads and navigable waterways.

♦ THE CEREMONIAL AREA OF TENOCHTITLAN
The Aztec capital was divided into districts. Four districts symbolized north, south, east, and west. A fifth, ceremonial, district symbolized the unity of earth and sky. Here a surrounding wall, decorated with serpent figures and measuring 984 feet (300 m) along each side, enclosed six pyramidal temples of varying sizes, a court for the sacred ball game (*tlachtli*), an altar for sacrifices, a pool for ritual baths, and also schools, a library, and the residences of the priests.

♦ A RITUAL IN THE HEART OF THE AZTEC CAPITAL
The Aztec emperor performed ritual dances in the central plaza of Tenochtitlan, where Mexico City stands today. Tenochtitlan was, in effect, the Aztec capital, full of bustling activity; and, like Amsterdam or Venice, it was a city of canals and bridges.

SACRED DANCES ♦
Dedicated to the goddesses of the earth, these dances lasted several hours. According to a cruel decree, anyone who missed a step was punished with death.

♦ **THE SUN CULT**
Many of the Aztecs'
temples were
dedicated to the sun.
The rituals were

♦ **THE SUN CULT**
Many of the Aztecs'
temples were
dedicated to the sun.
The rituals were
performed at the foot
of the temple, because
only the priests were
permitted to approach
the divinity.

♦ **BUILDING
MATERIALS**
The pyramids were
made with sun-dried
bricks, faced with
stone, which was
given a protective
coating of plaster.
Unlike abandoned
Mayan monuments
in the jungle, Aztec
buildings were
systematically
destroyed by the
Spanish, leaving only
some scattered ruins.

THE RENAISSANCE

The Renaissance, a profound change in existing human values, began in 14th-century Italy and later spread over most of Europe. In the arts, and especially in architecture, it was based on the rediscovery and systematic study of the works of classical (ancient Greek and Roman) antiquity, which was regarded as an unsurpassed model of what civilization should be. Harmony, symmetry, and regularity were seen as the classical ideals, and during the Renaissance it became possible to understand and exercise full control over the arrangement and proportions of buildings, thanks to Renaissance achievements in the scientific study of perspective and the mastery of geometry. These were the instruments used by architects to reinterpret the classical style and apply it to contemporary problems of building and urban planning. In the early 15th century, the wealthy city-state of Florence became the center of the new movement. The greatest architectural achievement of the time was the dome of Florence Cathedral, designed by Filippo Brunelleschi.

✦ THE CRADLE OF THE RENAISSANCE

At the beginning of the 15th century the merchant aristocracy in Italy achieved unprecedented levels of wealth and power. This was true above all in Florence, where the republican constitution remained in force but a banking and mercantile family, the Medici, dominated the government. The Medici lavished patronage on writers and artists, and promoted grand public works to enhance their prestige. An additional motive was provided by the intense competition between the Italian states for cultural supremacy. In this ferment, extensive building operations were undertaken in Florence, and some of the greatest Renaissance artists worked in the city, including Masaccio, Brunelleschi (above), and Alberti, and later Leonardo and Michelangelo. A treatise by the Roman architect Vitruvius, *De Architectura*, served as the main model for architects, supplemented in the late 15th century by *De Re Aedificatoria*, by Leon Battista Alberti (1404–72), in which the practices of classical architects were recorded and codified as a set of rules. Later still, Andrea Palladio (1508–80) expanded the classical tradition in his buildings, and in writings which remained influential to the 19th century.

✦ FLORENCE CATHEDRAL

Begun in 1296 by Arnolfo di Cambio, this was an enormous construction site for a century and a half. The campanile (bell tower) was built by the painter Giotto, who was appointed master builder in 1334. However, it was only in 1418 that the project for the huge dome was approved. Brunelleschi won the commission and work on the dome started in 1420.

✦ SANTA MARIA NOVELLA

Designed and built by Leon Battista Alberti between 1456 and 1470, the façade is a clear example of his conception of beauty. It was raised above pointed (Gothic) arches, visible in the lower section. Alberti added a pediment, columns, pilasters, and two scrolling features (volutes), designed to conceal the irregular skyline of the Gothic church behind. The result was a dignified design in line with Renaissance ideas.

✦ PALAZZO MEDICI-RICCARDI

This was designed by Michelozzo (1396–1472), the great architect of Medici dwellings. Built around a square courtyard, it has a three-story façade, with rows of identical windows on the upper floors. The regular, formal arrangement and clean lines are exemplary.

BEEHIVE STRUCTURE ✦

To cover an octagonal area 140 feet (43 m) in diameter, Brunelleschi designed a double dome supported by eight large ribs. There were a further two intermediate ribs for each segment, reinforced with horizontal arches. The hollow space between the outer and inner domes reduced the weight that had to be borne.

THE MASONRY ✦

The lower part of the dome is built with blocks of stone, and the upper part with bricks. The interlocking herringbone arrangement made the blocks self-supporting at every stage of building, so huge and expensive central supports were not needed.

**A SYMBOL OF ♦
THE CITY**
The drum and dome
of the cathedral are in
proportion, not with
the width of the
building, but rather
with the surrounding
landscape. The
cathedral can be seen
even from the hills
around Florence, and
is now a landmark and
symbol of the city.

**♦ FILIPPO
BRUNELLESCHI**
(1377–1446)
Brunelleschi derived
the elements of
his architectural
vocabulary from the
buildings of classical
antiquity, blending
them with
extraordinary
freedom and skill.
It was he who
developed the science
of perspective,
applied by Alberti to
architectural theory.
This enabled artists
and architects to
define and illustrate
with the greatest
precision, in the two
dimensions of a sheet
of paper, the shapes
and proportions of
objects in three-
dimensional space.
Thus, thanks to the
use of perspective,
it was possible to
record an existing
space, if the
measurements
involved were known,
so that it was easier
to study: and, of
course, it became
possible to draw an
accurate outline of
a structure that had
not yet been built.
In his own work
Brunelleschi took
responsibility for
planning both the
parts and the whole,
thus breaking with
the medieval tradition
of collective work
done by specialized
craftsmen.
Brunelleschi was
always present at the
construction site and
it was he who trained
his workmen. Among
his other famous
works were San
Lorenzo, Santa Maria
degli Angeli, Santo
Spirito, the Ospedale
degli Innocenti, and
the Pazzi Chapel
(above), all in
Florence.

♦ THE DOME
The dome has eight
elegantly curved
white marble ribs and
is covered with red
tiles. The vigorous
thrust toward the sky
recalls the Gothic
style, but the
engineering, and the
overall impression
created by the
rhythm of the
surfaces and colors,
is that of a new age.

**♦ THE DRUM AND
THE CROSSING**
The drum and dome
are raised above the
crossing, where the
transept and the main
body of the cathedral
meet. The ends of
the transept and the
chancel are rounded
like apses and are
covered with part-
octagonal domes.
The round windows
in the drum allow in
plenty of light.

CITY PLANNING

In medieval Europe, castles and monasteries often attracted settlement, forming the nuclei of new towns. But the towns themselves were of limited importance until the 10th century, when trade and urban life began to flourish again. In most places, city centers grew up around buildings such as the cathedral, the town hall, the covered market, and the local monastic church. Italian towns flourished earlier than towns in other parts of Europe, but their size was restricted by their surrounding walls and, for a long time, the only way in which the rapidly growing urban population could be housed was by increasing the height of existing buildings. From the 15th century the most prosperous Italian cities were embellished with buildings in the Renaissance style, and during this period architects also became interested in designing ideal cities. This activity anticipated the development of the practical art of town planning, though very few examples of even partial schemes on any great scale were actually executed. One such was Pienza, the center of which was rebuilt on the orders of Pope Pius II.

♦ THE BIRTH OF
TOWN PLANNING
In his treatise
De Architectura,
the Roman architect
Vitruvius described
an ideal city that was
circular in plan, with
the forum and the
main public buildings
in the center.
Many Renaissance
artists drew their
inspiration from this
authoritative work.
Filarete (1400–60)
drew up plans for
a city dedicated to
Francesco Sforza:
the star-shaped plan
visualized a circle
of canals and roads
linking town squares,
buildings, walls,
and gates. Aesthetic
problems and utopian
solutions to them
were not the only
matters considered
by Filarete, who
tackled questions
of hygiene, social
activities, production,
and administration.
Leonardo da Vinci
studied traffic
problems during his
stay in Milan, and he
made the first detailed
topographical map of
the city of Imola.
At Ferrara, Duke
Ercole d'Este and
his architect Biagio
Rossetti conceived
and brought about a
radical reorganization
of the city between
1493 and 1510. In the
new part of Ferrara,
wide paved roads
were laid out
regularly, lined by
the brick walls of the
long, low buildings
beside them. The
center was conceived
as a crossroads.
Michelangelo
designed a new plan
for the Capitoline Hill
in Rome, which was
executed after his
death. Above:
Rossetti's Palazzo dei
Diamanti, Ferrara.

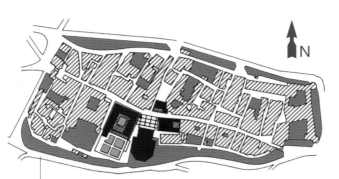

♦ PLAN FOR PIENZA
The rural settlement
of Corsignano was
transformed into the
papal town of Pienza.
It is situated on a hill
and overlooks the
Val d'Orcia, not far
from Siena.

The old main road
bends as it runs
past the square,
and this prevented
Rossellino from
orienting the new
buildings so that they
stood at right angles
to one another.

AENEAS SILVIUS ♦
PICCOLOMINI
(1405–64)
Piccolomini was a
refined intellectual
and patron of the arts.
In 1458 he became
pope, taking the
name Pius II.

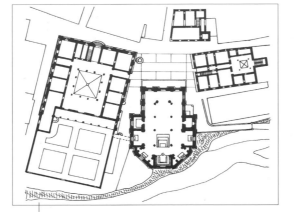

♦ THE PLAN: DETAIL
Following Pope Pius
II's orders, Rossellino
redesigned the entire
city center: not only
the cathedral, but also
the bishop's palace on

the left, the town hall
on the right, the
square, and the
existing roads.
However, he did not
radically change the
medieval layout.

♦ PIENZA
When the humanist
Aeneas Silvius
Piccolomini
became pope, he
transformed his
native village into
the city of Pienza.
In 1459 he
commissioned
Bernardo Rossellino,
who had trained
under Alberti, to
build an imposing
city center.

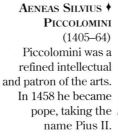

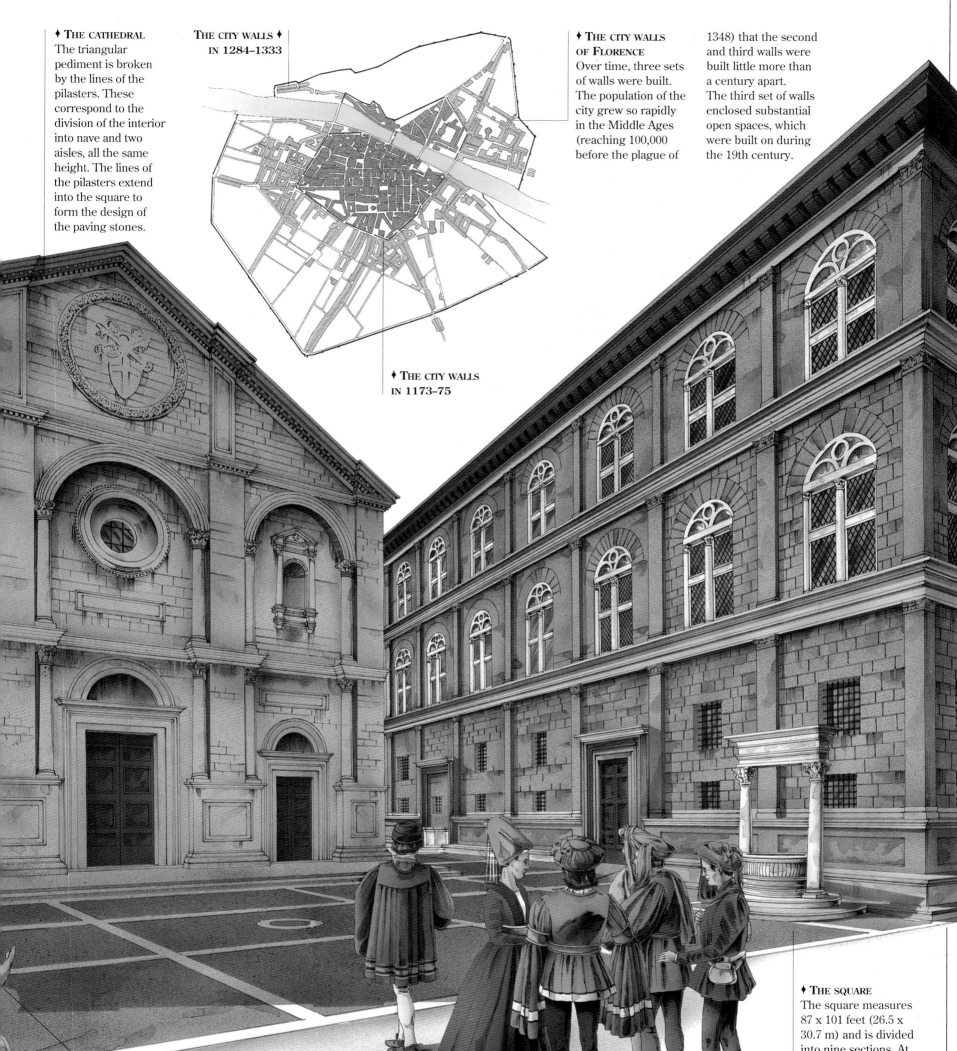

♦ THE CATHEDRAL
The triangular
pediment is broken
by the lines of the
pilasters. These
correspond to the
division of the interior
into nave and two
aisles, all the same
height. The lines of
the pilasters extend
into the square to
form the design of
the paving stones.

THE CITY WALLS ♦
IN 1284–1333

**♦ THE CITY WALLS
OF FLORENCE**
Over time, three sets
of walls were built.
The population of the
city grew so rapidly
in the Middle Ages
(reaching 100,000
before the plague of
1348) that the second
and third walls were
built little more than
a century apart.
The third set of walls
enclosed substantial
open spaces, which
were built on during
the 19th century.

**♦ THE CITY WALLS
IN 1173–75**

**♦ BERNARDO
ROSSELLINO**
(1409–64)
Sculptor and architect
Rossellino completed
the lantern of
Brunelleschi's dome,
and built the Palazzo
Rucellai, in Florence,
designed by Alberti.

♦ THE SQUARE
The square measures
87 x 101 feet (26.5 x
30.7 m) and is divided
into nine sections. At
one side is a well.
The cathedral façade
is on one of the long
sides of the square.
The building on the
right is the Palazzo
Piccolomini.

ON THE WATER

From the 6th century A.D., citizens from mainland Italy, in flight from the political and military upheavals of the time, began to settle permanently in an area of islands and lagoons on the Adriatic coast. Within a few centuries of this humble beginning, the largest trading center in Europe developed on the site: Venice, a unique example of a city built on the water, among winding canals. Layers of clay and sand were laid down and stakes were driven into the mud flats to stabilize them; the channels between the islands were bridged; and stone houses of increasing grandeur were raised on the foundations created by close-packed piles driven into the swampy soil. Timbers were installed at strategic points in the buildings, helping to create a flexible response to strains and cope with subsidence. The Venetians' need to exploit every possible area for building is exemplified by the Rialto Bridge.

♦ THE SHOPS
Once the structure was complete, work was begun on the construction of two rows of 24 shops about 18 feet (4.5 m) wide. The slender pillars and wide arches made them particularly light. In the center two high arches give views of the Grand Canal.

♦ DECORATIVE FEATURES
Unlike the rest of the structure, the decorative features, added later, were executed specifically in the Renaissance style. They include the 27-inch (70-cm) high cornice crowning the single arch of the bridge.

THE PIER ♦
A mass of masonry supports the bridge. It is 33.5 feet (10.2 m) wide and 75.5 feet (23 m) long, and is built with 5,000 blocks of stone, bricks, and lime mortar of the best quality, which came from the nearby town of Padua. Materials such as wood and metal recovered from ancient ruins were also used to build the bridge.

♦ THE RIALTO BRIDGE
The 16th-century bridge was built by craftsmen, directed by Antonio da Ponte. He was a relatively obscure figure whose design for the bridge had been chosen in preference to those of more distinguished architects who would have imposed a more overtly Renaissance-classical style. The choice of da Ponte was perhaps a victory for pragmatism.

♦ **THE FLOATING CONSTRUCTION SITE**
Venice's naval dockyard provided a barge that moored under the bridge and was used as a construction yard.

♦ **THE RIALTO DISTRICT**
The Rialto district is located on the island where the first Venetian settlement took place. Overlooking the right bank of the Grand Canal, it was for centuries the commercial heart of the republic. The bridge linking it with the rest of the city burned down in 1514, and the stalls of the market that originally stood on the bridge were destroyed with it. The Venetian government took over 70 years, during which many designs were put forward, to begin building a new bridge.

♦ **BRIDGES THROUGH HISTORY**
The first wooden bridges, made of beams placed across a watercourse, date back to 4000 B.C. The arched bridge originated in Mesopotamia and was developed greatly by the Romans. The bas-relief on Trajan's Column depicts a bridge built over the Danube, the longest in antiquity (1 mile, or 1.6 km), with wooden arches resting on stone piers. In the Middle Ages, the Church, which had preserved some knowledge of Roman techniques, directed bridge-building, and special orders of friars (*fratres pontifices*) were founded for that purpose. They were responsible for the construction of bridges in Avignon and London at the end of the 14th century. During the Renaissance bridge-building again became a feat of civil engineering and was also subject to aesthetic considerations. The harmonious three-arched bridge of Santa Trinità in Florence and the Pont-Neuf in Paris, both in stone, belong to the 16th century. In the 18th century, bridge-building became the province of the engineer, and in 1747 the first school of engineering was founded. From the 19th century the introduction of new materials has made it possible to build very long suspension bridges such as the Golden Gate in San Francisco (above)

♦ **THE PALAZZO DEI CAMERLENGHI**
Built with stone from Istria between 1525 and 1528, this dazzling white palazzo is a highly ornamented example of the Renaissance style. It replaced an earlier building destroyed in the fire of 1514. The Camerlenghi were the financial officials of the Venetian Republic, and the palazzo was one of the first buildings of such a size in Europe to be used exclusively for offices.

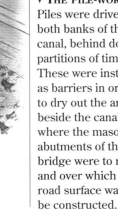

♦ **THE PILE-WORK**
Piles were driven into both banks of the canal, behind double partitions of timber. These were installed as barriers in order to dry out the areas beside the canal where the masonry abutments of the bridge were to rest and over which the road surface was to be constructed.

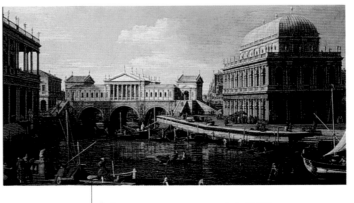

♦ **AN ALTERNATIVE DESIGN**
A design for the Rialto Bridged proposed by Andrea Palladio in the late 1560s was more in Renaissance style, with columns, three arches, and a pavilion on the highest point.

AGAINST EARTHQUAKES

In the many islands that make up Japan, human beings never dwelt in caves or rock shelters. Even during the Stone Age they built huts among greenery, close to rivers and in forests. Despite the cold climate, the Japanese developed light, open-plan buildings, using wood, present in abundance, as their main material. The apparent fragility of Japanese buildings is actually an advantage: flexible materials such as wood and bamboo withstand or bend to the force of the frequent earthquakes and cyclones; and even when completely destroyed, such structures can easily be rebuilt. In addition, the nature of the materials creates a harmonious relationship between buildings and landscape.

♦ THE TEA CEREMONY
The tea ceremony is a meditation ritual, introduced by the Zen masters. The need for a special room in which it could take place led to the construction of simple and secluded buildings, and these influenced later domestic architecture.

♦ THE KATSURA IMPERIAL VILLA
Built on an isolated site southwest of Kyoto, in the heart of Japan, the Katsura imperial villa is an early-17th-century masterpiece of architecture. In the garden surrounding the villa there are five pavilions, which are used for the tea ceremony.

THE FUNCTION ♦ OF THE VILLA
The villa is one of the country homes of a noble Japanese family, greatly extended to provide peace and tranquillity for visitors. The original building was based on a parlor and reading room, with a bathroom and kitchen attached. In the space of a few decades a new reading and meditation room, a music wing, and a residential area were added.

♦ THE INTERIOR
The interior is divided up by movable screens. Large windows open onto verandas, which provide a natural transition from the covered area to the garden around it.

THE ZEN GARDEN ✦

A Zen garden is a place of meditation. Its elements are intended to suggest rather than literally represent a landscape, which will be completed in the mind of the beholder. The garden's main features are pebbles or unusual rock forms set in areas of raked sand and gravel.

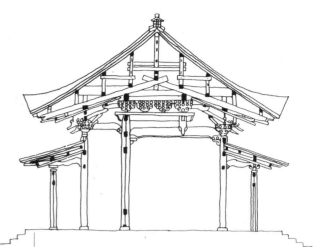

✦ THE SHOFUKUJI TEMPLE

Zen Buddhism became established in Japan in the 12th and 13th centuries. Its austerity and discipline had a particular appeal to the Samurai warrior elite of Japan. Zen masters taught meditation as a thought-free discipline and were celebrated for asking unanswerable questions in order to disrupt the logical processes of their pupils' minds and produce a flash of enlightenment. Built in 1195, the Shofukuji temple was the earliest Zen temple in Japan.

✦ THE STRUCTURE

The palace is built with natural wood, which absorbs or releases moisture according to weather conditions, thus maintaining a stable, healthy environment.

✦ TRADITION

Japan's architectural tradition emphasizes the integration of buildings with the natural environment. Houses tend to be modest in scale and made of natural materials such as wood and thatch or shingle. Even larger dwellings like the Katsura imperial villa have this simplicity and naturalness.

BAROQUE

In the 17th century, challenged by the rise of the nation-state and Protestantism, the papacy asserted itself, erecting monuments to the grandeur of the Catholic Church, filled with compelling religious imagery. Spectacular building schemes transformed the "Eternal City," Rome, into the greatest of all European capitals. The basis for this had been laid between 1585 and 1590, after Pope Sixtus V ordered the construction of a new road system linking the principal churches, with fountains and obelisks strategically placed to serve as landmarks for pilgrims. Seventeenth-century architects worked in a new style, the Baroque, which reinterpreted Renaissance classicism in terms of space and drama. The city was turned into an enormous stage, where the arts and architecture were combined to produce spectacles of great variety. An example is the Piazza Navona, where the fountains, palaces, and churches form a panoramic vista which can be enjoyed from countless different viewpoints.

♦ **FROM RENAISSANCE TO BAROQUE**
In the first half of the 16th century, Michelangelo's work as an architect pointed the way forward from the symmetry and static grandeur of Renaissance design. In the Medici Chapel (above) and the Laurentian Library in Florence, he showed how a building could be treated as an organism in which the structural and decorative elements were effectively merged. The classical ideals of harmony and balance were rejected in favor of artifice and effects of movement. Baroque architects took these ideas much further. To them, space was where human events were enacted, and therefore it was dynamic and could be manipulated for expressive effect. They harnessed all the arts, exploiting the colors of materials, and even natural elements such as water and light, to create overwhelming works that would affect all the senses of the spectators. Baroque architecture was fully developed in Rome by Gianlorenzo Bernini (1598–1680), who designed the great colonnade in St. Peter's Square, and by his pupil and rival Francesco Borromini (1599–1667). The style became dominant at the Catholic courts of Europe and was taken by the Jesuits to Central and South America.

♦ **THE SQUARE**
This was almost entirely reconstructed around 1650, but it retains the elongated form of the stadium built there by the Roman Emperor Domitian. There is a fountain near each end, and a third, the famous Fountain of the Four Rivers, in the center. The winding streets of the medieval town, with their tall, narrow houses, lead away in all directions.

♦ **THE FOUNTAIN OF THE FOUR RIVERS**
Created by Bernini between 1648 and 1651, the fountain's stonework is carved to represent rocks, with four colossal figures at the corners and a Roman obelisk rising from the center. The figures represent the Danube, Ganges, Nile, and Plate Rivers, signifying the four quarters of the globe.

SANT'AGNESE ♦
The church was designed to be admired from the many viewpoints provided by the long, narrow square. The façades of Baroque churches no longer reflected the internal organization but were dramatic statements, gaining significance from their relationship to nearby buildings.

♦ **PALAZZO PAMPHILI**
The palazzo was built from the late 1640s by Girolamo Rinaldi, for the Pamphili Pope Innocent X. Like several earlier popes, Innocent was determined to leave glorious monuments in stone to his family's greatness. Rinaldi designed the building so that the features of its façade would match those of the college and library on the other side of the domed church of Sant'Agnese.

SAN GIACOMO ♦ DEGLI SPAGNOLI
This was the head-quarters of the Spanish friars, who organized festivals in the piazza.

♦ **THE PIAZZA NAVONA, ROME**
Like a permanent stage set, the Piazza Navona was flooded for mock naval battles, as well as hosting festivals. A festival in 1675 marked the Church's 15th Jubilee .

♦ **DECORATION**
To make the area even more spectacular, the piazza was surrounded by a colonnade, which was decked with greenery and had 1,600 torches placed along it.

THE FAÇADE OF ♦ SANT'AGNESE
The façade of Sant'Agnese, by Borromini, is dressed entirely in travertine stone, and its projections and recesses create strong contrasts between light and shadow. Two towering but elegant belfries provide a setting for the dome, which rests on a very tall drum. The drum's boldly projecting pilasters are separated by large windows.

THE FORBIDDEN CITY

The imperial Chinese city of Beijing (Peking) was crossed from south to north by a grand processional road, which passed through the gates of a series of city walls. This was because Beijing consisted of three walled cities, one within the other, as well as a market area for the common people, called the "Chinese city," to the south. The outermost walled area, 15 miles (24 km) in circumference, was known as the Tartar City because it originated during a period of Mongol rule; it housed the nobles and officials. Then came the Imperial City, filled with parks, artificial lakes, temples, and secondary palaces. Finally, through the Meridian Gate, lay the moated Forbidden City, a huge rectangular area housing the emperor and his wives and concubines. Only favored courtiers and servants were allowed to enter the Forbidden City. White marble steps and terraces led along its main axis to the Hall of Supreme Harmony, which held the emperor's golden throne. This was the center of a complex of audience halls, palaces, temples, and libraries, all dedicated to the use of the semidivine ruler, known as the "Son of Heaven."

♦ **THE FRAME**
A complex arrangement of beams and brackets enabled the Chinese to build roofs with distinctive curves. The cantilevered brackets above the columns supported the projecting roof edge. The cornices were carved with the imperial dragon symbol.

♦ **THE HALL OF SUPREME HARMONY**
At the center of the Forbidden City is the hall where the emperor and the court assembled on occasions such as the New Year and the emperor's birthday. 115 feet (35 m) high and built on a marble base with wide staircases, it is the largest timber-framed building in China.

♦ **MATERIALS**
All the buildings in the Forbidden City are supported by timber frames, made from trees which were brought by river from a province 900 miles (1,500 km) away. By the Ming era, deforestation threatened the entire basis of the Chinese architectural tradition, and in later centuries more slender elements had to be employed.

♦ **THE PLAN** ♦
Within the moat lies the Forbidden City, a vast rectangular area (250 acres; 100 hectares) in the heart of Beijing. The public offices are located along the central axis. Behind the Hall of Supreme Harmony (1) lies the smaller Hall of Central Harmony (2), where the emperor prepared himself for the performance of state rituals. The Hall of the Preservation of Harmony (3) is where foreign dignitaries were received.

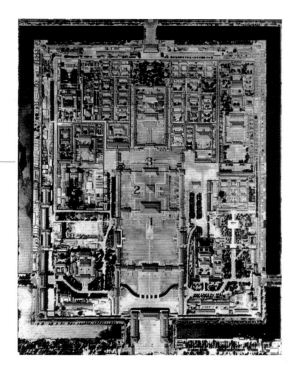

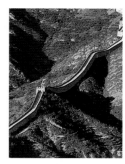

♦ **CHINA**
Chinese civilization was already old when its feudal phase ended and the rival Chinese states were conquered by the first emperor, Shih Huang Di, late in the 3rd century B.C. The emperor began the construction of the famous Great Wall of China (above), to protect the empire from attacks by nomadic peoples to the north. Reinforced and extended over the centuries, the wall was ultimately 4,000 miles (6,400 km) long. Shih Huang Di's draconian policies made his dynasty unpopular, and it was short-lived; but the succeeding Han dynasty (206 B.C.–A.D. 221) consolidated his achievements. Imperial China was most powerful during the Tang era (618–906), but reached its artistic zenith under the Song (960–1279), celebrated for its exquisite porcelain and scroll paintings. The transfer of the capital to Beijing was the work of Kublai Khan, during the period of Mongol rule in the 13th and 14th centuries. After the expulsion of the Mongols, the Ming dynasty ruled from 1368 to 1644, during which time the city was divided into three distinct walled areas: the Outer City, where most of the population lived; the Imperial City, with palaces and gardens; and, in the center, the Forbidden City, an imperial palace complex of thousands of chambers.

♦ **THE ROOF**
The roof is supported by solid wooden columns coated with red lacquer, and it is covered with yellow tiles. The effect is dazzling.

THE EMPEROR ♦
The role of the "Son of Heaven" was to preserve harmony between the human, natural, and spiritual worlds.

ROYAL PALACES

Most European countries in the 17th and 18th centuries were ruled by absolute monarchs, whose sovereign will was almost unbridled. One expression of this was a Western version of China's Forbidden City – a royal palace, isolated from the masses, from which the monarch governed the realm. The prototype and largest example was the palace of Versailles in France, where building went on for almost a century. In scale and almost everything else, it differed from the Italian city-states, the seats of the small German princes, and the stately homes of the aristocracy in the English countryside. Originally a hunting lodge, Versailles was transformed by Louis XIV, the Sun King, into the capital of his kingdom. Covering an area as large as Paris at that time, it was both miniature city and royal park. Such was Louis' prestige that, during the 18th century, European rulers great and small built themselves residences in imitation of Versailles.

♦ **VERSAILLES**
In 1682, fifteen years after work had begun on extending the hunting lodge south-west of Paris, Louis XIV transferred the government and court to Versailles. Work inside the palace, in the park, and in the adjacent village went on for several decades, but the new center of French power was already functioning, and the courtyards, halls, and gardens were filled with nobles, officials, and attendants.

♦ **THE PALACE**
The palace spreads over a vast area on either side of the former hunting lodge of Louis XIII. Designed by Le Vau and Jules Hardouin Mansart, the palace became a stage on which public and private ambitions, work, pleasure, and entertainment came together.

♦ **THE PARK**
The park around Versailles was designed by Le Nôtre, the leading landscape gardener of the age. A precisely laid out network of avenues and walks branches out from the main axis, eventually leading into the hills and woods, where the king went hunting.

✦ THE HALL OF MIRRORS
45 feet (72 m) long, this hall was used for public ceremonies and sumptuous balls during the reign of the Sun King. Seventeen windows face seventeen mirrors, which reflect spectacular views of the gardens.

✦ ROYAL RESIDENCES OF THE 18TH CENTURY
The kings of France resided mainly in the châteaux of the Loire until 1582, when they moved to Paris. The old palace of the Louvre was rebuilt, and early in the 17th century important public works were put in hand.
Louis XIV came to the throne as a child, and, during the insecure early years of his reign, Paris was a major center of disaffection. The threat posed by the city, and the desire to create an environment in which he could turn his nobles into servile courtiers, were important motives for building Versailles.
Imitations of the Sun King's palace appeared at an early date. In 1690, the Habsburg emperors started building the palace of Schönbrunn outside Vienna. In 1752 Carlo, the king of Naples, commissioned the architect Vanvitelli to build the palace of Caserta; later, as King Charles III of Spain, he rebuilt the royal palace in Madrid (shown above). Despite changes of style and technique, the influence of Versailles was apparent in the design of both palaces.
Many minor 18th-century rulers, especially in Germany, also built themselves miniature versions of Versailles.

✦ THE GARDENS
The gardens unfold, one after the other, among tall hedges, artificial grottoes, temples, open-air theaters, and fountains. Seen from the park, the western façade of the palace, 1,970 feet (600 m) long, fills the horizon; and from far away it still looks spectacular.

✦ A NEW TOWN
The small town of Versailles is very close to the palace. Under Louis XIV, it was rebuilt in order to house the court officials. The roads leading to the palace were turned into wide boulevards converging on the main square.

PALLADIANISM

After the Baroque era, with its illusionism, indulgence in fantasy, and spectacular effects, there was a reaction in favor of harmony and restrained elegance. The art of classical antiquity was more fully understood and more accurately used as a model than during the Renaissance, so that architecture during the 18th-century Age of Enlightenment became based on a combination of archeological research and rationalism. Its ultimate fruit was the movement known as Neoclassicism, but this was anticipated in England by a form of classicism known as Palladianism – inspired by the buildings and writings of the 16th-century Italian architect Andrea Palladio. In the United States, too, the Palladian style was extensively adopted, especially in the post-independence period. Examples of the style are found on Capitol Hill, in the White House, and in the University of Virginia designed by Thomas Jefferson.

♦ **THE COMPLEX**
The university complex consists of two groups of five porticoed pavilions, linked by colonnades running through a large grassy expanse.

♦ **THE UNIVERSITY OF VIRGINIA**
Thomas Jefferson (1743–1826) was the third president of the United States of America (1801–9) and an architect of very considerable ability. He designed the University of Virginia campus in Charlottesville, chartered in 1819 and opened in 1825.

♦ **THE PAVILIONS**
Each of the pavilions contained accommodation for a professor and a classroom. Each was designed by Jefferson in a different style, exemplifying a variation on known classical forms.

VILLA ALMERICO ♦
Better known as La Rotonda, this villa was built in 1550 by Andrea Palladio. It stands, temple-like, on a hill outside Vicenza and, with its four identical porticoes, dominates the countryside from all directions. Jefferson was influenced by it when he built his own mansion at Monticello, Virginia.

♦ ANDREA PALLADIO
(1508–80) Born in Padua of humble origins, Palladio was the first great professional architect. He learned from the writings of Vitruvius, and by studying the ruins of Roman buildings. To the principles of harmony and proportion that he adopted from Renaissance architecture, he added an erudition and characteristic smoothness of his own, and so the buildings he designed were both monumental and light and elegant. They include many mansions and a "Roman" theater, the Teatro Olimpico (above), in Vicenza. In the 1550s Palladio developed his own formula for the ideal villa. Based on a symmetrical plan, it had a central block, entered via a portico crowned with a pediment. Long wings consisting of farm buildings reached out on either side of the façade, helping to integrate the villa with the landscape. The rational and apparently simple nature of the Palladian style gave it a special appeal to 18th-century taste. This was especially true in Britain, where the first English edition (1730) of Palladio's treatise, the *Four Books of Architecture*, influenced the building of many country houses for the aristocracy and gentry. A few decades later, wealthy landowners in the southern states of the USA followed suit.

♦ THE "ROTUNDA"
The "Rotunda" dominates the landscape, standing at the far end of a large meadow which is flanked by several buildings. It is typically Palladian, with a central plan and a dome. A hexastyle (six-columned) portico leads into the villa, which has three oval rooms and a superb circular library.

♦ STUDENTS IN THE SUN
Jefferson's design allows for both study and open-air activity, very much in accordance with American educational ideas.

IRON AND STEEL

During the 19th century, the effects of the Industrial Revolution and the application of new technology changed the look of Western cities and the way people lived. New types of building appeared, such as factories and railroad stations, and new processes and mass-production techniques made it practicable to employ materials like iron, sheet glass, and, later, steel. From 1851, when the Great Exhibition was held in London, universal exhibitions became showcases for scientific progress, and the exhibition buildings themselves were architecturally significant as examples of improved techniques. This was especially true of the Crystal Palace in London, a light and luminous structure expressing new values, at a time when much contemporary architecture was still imitating the styles of the past.

♦ IRON BUILDINGS
The development of the iron and steel industries and new techniques of glass manufacture made it possible to raise an entirely new type of structure. Prefabricated iron rods could be put in place immediately to serve as a framework, on which sheets of glass could be hung.
As in Gothic cathedrals, the strength of the framework meant that the walls had no load-bearing function (curtain walls). Such buildings could be very large and strong, and yet admit large amounts of natural light. Combinations of iron, stone, and bricks made it possible to build exhibition pavilions, covered markets (such as the now-replaced Les Halles in Paris), railroad stations, and capacious warehouses. There was little resistance to such places associated with industry or practical transactions being built with new materials. On the other hand, buildings that were held to be "architecture" were thought to be incomplete unless they were traditional in style and materials.
Iron-frame construction reached its height during the Paris Exhibition of 1889, with the completion of two remarkable iron and steel structures: the Eiffel Tower (shown under construction, above) and the huge, glass-covered Galerie des Machines, the forerunner of all later hangars.

♦ THE DESIGNER
Sir Joseph Paxton (1803–65) was not a professional architect but the head gardener of the Duke of Devonshire, for whom he built large greenhouses. These were the prototypes of his Crystal Palace.

♦ THE CRYSTAL PALACE
The first Universal Exhibition was held in Hyde Park, London, in 1851. The iron and glass Crystal Palace was designed specifically for the occasion.

Over 6 million visitors admired the latest scientific, technological, and artistic works from all over the world. There were over 7,000 items from Britain and its empire, and 6,000 from other countries.

♦ ROOFED OVER
Extending over 20
acres (8 hectares),
the gigantic structure
was built on three
levels and featured
a great semicircular
transept rising to a
height of 108 feet
(33 m). On display
were all kinds of
items, from precision
tools to furniture.

**THE BIBLIOTHEQUE ♦
NATIONALE, PARIS**
Built in the 1860s by
Henri Labrouste, the
reading room and
stack rooms of the
national library were
remarkable because
the architect boldly
used iron instead of
stone for features

such as the columns
supporting the vaults.
At the time, such a
breach with tradition
was highly unusual;
but Labrouste had, in
fact, used the same
technique even
earlier, for the Library
of Sainte Geneviève
in Paris (1843–50).

♦ THE DECORATION
The architect Owen
Jones (1809–74)
designed the
decorations for inside
the Crystal Palace.
Having eliminated
ornamental details,
which would have
weighed down the
structure, he used

vivid colors to create
a bright and airy
atmosphere. Red flags
were hung from the
galleries, bearing the
names of exhibiting
countries. The outside
of the building was
predominantly white
or stone-colored, with
blue detailing.

TOWARD THE SKIES

In the 1880s, the first skyscrapers were built in North American cities. They first appeared in any numbers in Chicago, since land was expensive there and owners therefore tried to exploit their lots to the maximum by building upward. Two inventions made it possible to build and inhabit these giants, which were to change the skylines of cities throughout the world. Steel allowed architects to design structures even stronger and lighter than iron-frame buildings; and the development of high-speed elevators enabled residents and workers to reach an apartment or office hundreds of feet above the ground in a very short time. The most famous city skyline dominated by skyscrapers is that of New York; concentrated in Manhattan, the buildings can be seen from very far away, notably by passengers who have crossed the Atlantic to the United States.

♦ THE SKYSCRAPER
This type of building owes its viability to technological innovations such as artificial lighting, air conditioning, water supply, and waste elimination systems. Among the advantages enjoyed by inhabitants of these modern towers is the shared use of facilities and services. The visual impact of the skyscraper is obvious, and the most famous American examples can also be regarded as huge advertisements for the corporations that had them built and made them their headquarters. New York's Empire State Building, shown above, was built between 1929 and 1931. At 1,250 feet (381 m) high, it was the world's tallest building, and remained so for 39 years; but its completion coincided with the Great Depression, as a result of which no one wanted to rent offices in it and it was nicknamed "the Empty State Building." But, even before the economy recovered, it was regarded as a marvel, much visited by out-of-town tourists. With the addition of a television tower in 1951, the Empire State Building reached a height of 1,472 feet (448 m).

♦ NEW YORK
During the 20th century, New York became the business and financial capital of the Western world. It was also a magnet for ambitious Americans and immigrants from overseas. During the course of the century, a million people arrived there by boat; the city teemed with people, its buildings soared, and New York became the center of frenetic activities that were only partly interrupted by the Great Depression of 1929.

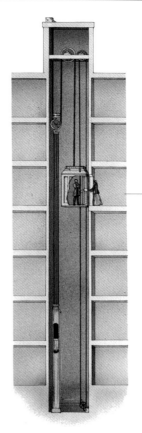

♦ THE ELEVATOR
The elevator was invented in 1852 by Elisha Otis (1811–61), an engineer from Vermont. The first elevators had a steam-operated hydraulic pump, which was later replaced by an electric motor. The first public elevator was installed in a department store in New York in 1857.

DEMOLITION ♦
Much of 19th-century New York was demolished in order to make room for tall new buildings. The traditional 4–5 floor "brownstone" houses are now becoming rare.

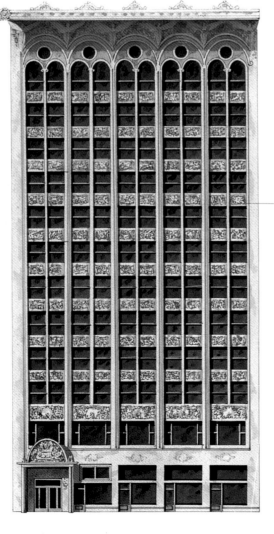

♦ THE BAYARD BUILDING
Built in 1898, this is the only work designed for New York by Louis Sullivan, a pioneer of metal-frame building based in Chicago. (The even more famous Frank Lloyd Wright trained under Sullivan.) The façade of the Bayard Building is notable for the rhythmic alternation of its thick and thin pilasters.

♦ THE FOUNDATIONS
The foundations of New York's skyscrapers rest on bedrock which is approximately 80 feet (25 m) deep.

♦ **THE WORKFORCE**
New York's sky-scrapers were built by a workforce made up of Native Americans and also new immigrants from the poorest areas of the Old World. Both were willing to work on scaffolding that rose to incredible, dizzy heights.

♦ **THE FLATIRON BUILDING**
Resembling a huge, old-fashioned iron, this was built in 1902, at the intersection of Fifth Avenue and Broadway, New York. It was the first free-standing skyscraper. Inside, a power plant supplied electric light, while steam was used for heating.

♦ **STYLES**
New York skyscrapers were built over a number of decades, and so the styles employed ranged from the Classical, as in the Flatiron Building, to Neo-Gothic and Art Deco.

PREFABRICATION

Sensational economic and technological developments in the 1950s and '60s had a remarkable influence on architecture. In this, as in other fields, policy-makers and planners felt able to act on an increasingly large scale, to the point where some disastrous ecological mistakes were made. Architects reacted in various ways to commissions for office buildings or residential complexes, placing their faith in new materials and confident that comfortable and functional environments could be created by ambitious and original schemes, without recourse to long-established building techniques and traditions. Some utopian schemes never left the drawing board, but occasionally they were carried through, thanks to new building procedures such as the prefabrication of entire apartment complexes. This has inevitably entailed repetition, and with it the risk of monotony; however, the aesthetic effect of these buildings, as with much 20th-century architecture, is produced by the interplay of masses and volumes rather than by the use of decorative detailing.

♦ **DRY ASSEMBLY**
Mass production makes it possible to manufacture components that can be assembled by interlocking, without cement. Over the last few decades, many solutions of this kind have been available, so that standardization can be combined with flexible and varied schemes of construction.

♦ **THE COMPLEX**
Apparently irregular, the Habitat '67 complex is based, in fact, on the distribution of rectangular units. The only exceptions are walkways leading to the various housing units across large terraces created by the protruding modules.

♦ **HABITAT '67**
Seventy nations took part in the 1967 Universal Exhibition (Expo '67), held in Montreal, Canada, and it was visited by 50 million people. The theme of the exhibition was "Man and his world." Particular attention was paid to the problems posed by the growing urbanization of the world's population. An entire village, Habitat '67, was built from prefabricated residential modules, interlocking in clusters.

MODULES ✦
Each housing unit, made from concrete, is a prefabricated box, ready to be integrated with others according to the master plan. The operation requires great accuracy and is carried out by a specially trained workforce.

✦ CRANES
Indispensable machines on the modern construction site, cranes can lift and shift extremely heavy loads. To assemble Habitat '67, it was necessary to use not only the standard types of crane but special rotary cranes whose arms were capable of moving more freely.

✦ LIGHT AND HEAVY PREFABRICATION
In a sense, architects have always assembled buildings with prefabricated elements, since the term can be applied to wooden beams, blocks of stone, or bricks. However, there was a revolution in building technology during the 20th century, with the introduction of new materials that were strong and flexible, and with the mass production of standardized single items. The use of these has made it possible for entire buildings to be designed as clusters of serially produced elements, thus keeping down costs and simplifying the work of the builders. This is known as light prefabrication. Later on, better transport facilities encouraged the development of heavy prefabrication, in which the elements to be assembled are larger and more complex – for example, entire blocks of foundations, walls, or roofing. The case of Habitat '67 shows that it is possible to go further, building apartments and then putting them together as desired, as if playing with a child's building blocks.

Above: concrete structures for underground piping.

✦ THE ARCHITECT
The architect was a young Israeli, Moshe Safdie. In 1968–71 he developed, but was unable to execute, plans for residential units in New York and Puerto Rico, based on his Montreal project.

MEGASTRUCTURES

After World War II, a faith in the unlimited potential of high technology led to architectural projects of unprecedented dimensions. Enormous buildings were designed, in which identical floors were constructed on the different levels, and in which living areas, commercial, educational, and managerial functions, leisure activities, and a range of services were all brought together in a single place. The great pioneer of this approach was the Swiss architect Le Corbusier. He realized that architecture would have to come to terms with the nature of the modern commercial and industrial metropolis, with its increased population density, and with sophisticated technology. Among the megastructures that resulted, some were organized as flexible structures that could be altered or enlarged at need. An outstanding example was the press and broadcasting center built in the late 1960s at Kofu in Japan.

♦ THE YAMANASHI PRESS AND BROADCASTING CENTER, KOFU
Designed by the Japanese architect Kenzo Tange, the Yamanashi Center was built on the slopes of Mount Fuji in 1966–67. It is a gigantic structure, raised on huge towers – a method of building that makes the architect's creation entirely independent of the terrain below it.

♦ THE COMMERZBANK, FRANKFURT
Completed in 1997, this skyscraper was designed by British architect Norman Foster. It is the tallest office building in Europe. Although intended exclusively for business purposes, it has remarkably generous and well-planned areas of greenery throughout, designed for common use and as reception areas for visitors.

♦ **UNITÉ D'HABITATION, MARSEILLES**
Completed in 1952, this can be considered the model for all megastructures. It was designed by Swiss architect Le Corbusier (1887–1965), one of the great masters of 20th-century architecture. It contains over 330 apartments, two stories of shops, and, on the roof terrace, a communal garden, a nursery school, a gymnasium, and a movie theater. The entire structure rests on pillars 26 feet (8 m) high. Le Corbusier hoped to build numerous complexes of this kind, distributed across a green landscape to form a "Radiant City."

♦ **THE INTERNATIONAL STYLE AND LATER DEVELOPMENTS**
Traditional styles of architecture continued to be important in the 20th century, and believers in a more functional and rational style had to struggle hard to find commissions. By the 1930s, this Modern or International style had achieved a certain prominence, with Walter Gropius, Le Corbusier, and Mies van der Rohe as its outstanding practitioners. But the rise of Nazism and World War II intervened, many modernist architects fled to the United States, and it was here that the International style first became dominant, after the war spreading all over the world. Characterized by the use of steel, reinforced concrete, and large areas of glass, but largely dispensing with decoration, International-style buildings seemed to be highly practical responses to the needs of mass society, and for several decades the style appeared to be the inevitable answer to any large-scale architectural problem. However, its air of austerity and sameness eventually provoked a reaction, and by the 1980s a "Postmodernist" trend was in evidence, readmitting fantasy and decoration to architecture. Above: façade of Le Corbusier's Unité d'Habitation.

♦ **MATERIALS**
As in much contemporary architecture, there is a prevalence of concrete, left in its original, rough state on external surfaces.

♦ **THE LAYOUT**
The television studios are situated on the upper floors, above the printing plant and all the offices.

♦ **A NEW TYPE OF STRUCTURE**
The system of supports consists, not of traditional elements, such as pillars and beams, but of hollow cylindrical towers. The different heights of the cylinders and their irregular arrangement create an impression of movement, as though the building is starting to grow upward.

THE 16 TOWERS ♦
16 feet (5 m) in diameter, these contain the stairs, the elevators, and the conduits for technical installations.

ORIGINAL SOLUTIONS

Functionalism and rationalism dominated architecture during the middle decades of the 20th century, when there was great enthusiasm for efficient and low-cost housing and huge, rectilinear office buildings. But eventually some architects began to seek greater formal and structural originality, for which opportunities most often arose in projects for prestigious public buildings such as museums, theaters, and galleries. A few architects, such as Frank Lloyd Wright and Jørn Utzon, took this path as early as the 1940s and '50s, when the functionalist International style was still the dominant force in architecture. The hold of the International style remained strong, and, even in the 1970s, the unusual appearance of the Pompidou Center in Paris, by Richard Rogers and Renzo Piano, aroused a good deal of controversy. However, within a few years, imaginative structures by architects such as Frank Gehry were winning almost universal acceptance.

♦ **THE KAUFMANN HOUSE**
This famous house, Falling Water, in Bear Run, Pennsylvania, was designed by Frank Lloyd Wright and built between 1936 and 1939. During the years when rationalism ruled, Wright created a structure that was integrated with nature: cantilevered out over a waterfall and built on rock which was allowed to thrust up into the house. The rooms flow into one another and into the landscape.

♦ **THE SYDNEY OPERA HOUSE**
This very modern opera house was designed by the Danish architect Jørn Utzon in 1956 and opened in 1973. As well as the operatic theater, it has a concert hall, a theater for drama, a movie theater, a library, two exhibition halls, and two restaurants. Thrusting out into Sydney Harbor like a gigantic ship in full sail, it has become a symbol of Australia.

♦ **THE KARL-MARX HOF COMPLEX**
In the 1920s, the municipality of Vienna sponsored several experiments in mass housing. Based on designs by leading architects, and inspired by socialist ideals, large blocks of working-class homes were built. The best known was the Karl-Marx Hof, a complex of hundreds of apartments designed by Karl Ehn and completed in 1929. Designed like a fortress around courtyards, it was in fact stormed and destroyed by extreme right-wing forces. Similar experiments were conducted in Berlin, Frankfurt, Amsterdam, and Rotterdam.

THE SHELL-VAULT ♦ ROOFS
These concrete vaults are covered with over a million shiny white ceramic tiles, arranged like fish scales. The tiles were manufactured in Sweden.

THE OPERATIC ♦ THEATER
Capable of seating 1,547 spectators, the theater has ideal acoustics for opera.

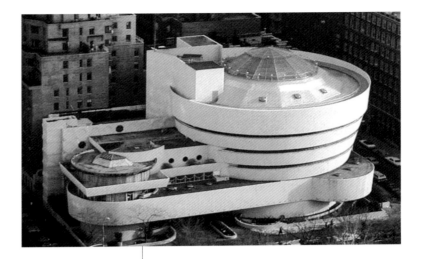

♦ POMPIDOU CENTER
Designed by Richard Rogers and Renzo Piano, the Pompidou Center is one of the great temples of contemporary culture. Built between 1971 and 1977 in the heart of Paris, it was structurally orthodox, but highly original at the time in placing all the technical elements and services (stairs, elevators, ducts) on the outside. This left more space inside for the display of exhibits and also gave the structure its futuristic appearance.

♦ MAXIMUM HEIGHT
The Opera House reaches 221 feet (67 m) high. Building it entailed considerable danger for the workers, because of the very steep sloping roofs and the smooth surfaces of the ceramic tiles.

♦ THE GUGGENHEIM MUSEUM, NEW YORK
In 1943, the philanthropist-collector Solomon Guggenheim asked Frank Lloyd Wright (1869–1959), one of the most original architects of the 20th century, to design this museum. Situated near Central Park, it has a unique design with a banded circular exterior and an interior spiral ramp, along which works of contemporary art are displayed. Completed in 1959, the museum soon became an attraction in its own right.

♦ THE CONCERT HALL
This is the largest hall in the entire complex and can seat 2,690 people. The ceiling's birch-wood lining was specially designed to enhance the acoustics for classical music.

♦ THE WALKWAY
The walkway unfolds around the building, creating a quaylike promenade.

♦ GLASS WINDOWS
Protected by the shell-shaped roofs, the windows are made of double layers of glass, to keep out the heat and noise of the harbor. The individual elements were made in France.

CONVERSION

Builders have long been in the habit of altering buildings, either to make them bigger, more comfortable, or more modern, or to adapt them to new functions. The latter motive has become particularly important in modern times, when many big-city buildings have lost their original purpose because of changes in living habits or technology. For example, in the capitals of Europe, there are still abandoned stations or factory complexes in what were once the suburbs. In some cases, buildings like these are real masterpieces of 19th- and 20th-century architecture, exemplifying various historic types of construction and styles; and it has now been realized that they should not be demolished but adapted to new needs and reutilized. A celebrated case is a 19th-century railroad station by the Seine River in Paris, the Gare d'Orsay, which was transformed in around 1980 into a museum which now houses the magnificent state collection of Impressionist and other 19th- and early-20th-century art.

♦ **THE GARE D'ORSAY**
The station was inaugurated for the Universal Exhibition in 1900 and was decommissioned in 1939. The museum was opened to the public in 1984.

THE BUILDING ♦
The original structure has been carefully restored. The vast ceiling of iron and glass provides strong natural lighting.

♦ **VIEW FROM THE OUTSIDE**
The architect Victor Leloux (1850–1937) concealed the building's industrial function behind a pompous stone façade. Inside, too, stone and stucco partly hide the bold use of metal and glass.

♦ **EXHIBITION AREAS**
An Italian architect, Gae Aulenti, was responsible for the new interior layout. It consists of a spacious, sloping concourse running down the center, partitioned areas leading off it, and displays on five levels above. There are also galleries in what was once the hotel attached to the station. The presentation of the exhibits emphasizes the social, as well as the aesthetic, history of art.

♦ **ARCHITECTURAL RESTORATION**
Restoration work is intended to reestablish the original state of a building that has been altered or that has suffered through time, war, or natural disasters. There are various types of restoration work. Conservation – preventing further deterioration – is done on buildings of historical or artistic value, such as great cathedrals. A different approach, possibly involving dismantling a structure and building it again, is used where there is a threat of collapse, for example through subsidence. Or a building that has disappeared may be reconstituted from the original materials, as at Ur. Another type of restoration consists of freeing a building of additions and alterations which have changed its original appearance. The reverse, the over-zealous restoration typical of the 19th century, meant finishing a building (or the decorative work on a building) that had long been left incomplete, by imitating the original style. Finally, as in the case of the Gare d'Orsay, innovative restoration involves devising a new function for a building. Above: the Malatesta Temple in Rimini, designed by Alberti, which became structurally unsafe and was dismantled and built again.

♦ **THE INTERIOR**
The new interior layout has been integrated with the existing architecture, thanks largely to the skillful matching of materials and colors.

TOWARD THE FUTURE

As the second millennium comes to an end, engineers and architects are faced with new challenges. One of these has arisen in Britain, which has decided to celebrate two thousand years of Western civilization by organizing a great exhibition. The theme is time, and the place is Greenwich, England, through which the meridian runs that is used to calculate time throughout the world. Four thousand years ago, humans erected the first colossal stone structures; two thousand years later, they had mastered the techniques of arch and dome construction; and slightly less than a thousand years ago, they were raising increasingly lofty cathedrals toward the sky. Today, modern technology makes it possible to manufacture light, strong materials that can be molded and assembled to build remarkably large structures with shapes at once simple and futuristic. Space and matter have seemingly been overcome; but time is still an elusive element. Only by looking at the extraordinary achievements of the past can we find the encouragement needed to tackle the even greater challenges of the future.

♦ **THE MILLENNIUM DOME**
This is a large structure erected at Greenwich, London, by the Thames River, to host the great exhibition organized in celebration of the year 2000. It has a diameter of 1,050 feet (320 m), is 164 feet (50 m) high, and can hold up to 100,000 visitors a day.

♦ **THE STRUCTURE**
Twelve tubular spars of colored metal, about 330 feet (100 m) high, serve to support the network of cables that keeps the structure in suspension and anchors it to the ground. The designer of the dome was the British architect Richard Rogers.

LIKE A CLOCK DIAL ♦
The surface of the dome is divided into 12 segments, corresponding to 12 pavilions on the ground floor. Each pavilion has a different theme. The opaque panels between the segments of the dome indicate the entrances into the building.

THE OTHER SPACES ♦
There are 12 spheres, each 66 feet (20 m) in diameter, around the circumference of the dome. These contain small auditoria and display areas. The spheres can be reached from the mezzanine level, where all the facilities (stores, bars, and restaurants) are found.

♦ THE COVERING
Made with Teflon,
a highly resistant
material, the
covering is divided
into 12 sectors by
opaque panels,

which also indicate
entrances to the
dome. Light
reflected by the
translucent Teflon
will be seen far
from London.

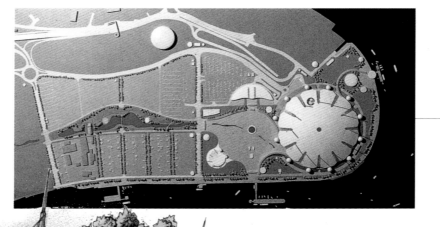

♦ VIEW FROM ABOVE
The model shows the
entire area that has
been set aside for
the exhibition.
Part of the area was
formerly occupied
by a gasometer.
New approaches by
land and water will
make the site highly
accessible.

♦ THE TAMBOUR
This is a glass wall
affording a view of
Meridian Gardens
and of the river.

◆ INDEX